NewMedia Magazine

Puzzle Workout

NewMedia Magazine

Puzzle Workout

A Multi-Dimensional
Exercise Program
for Your Mind

Scott Kim

RANDOM HOUSE
ELECTRONIC PUBLISHING

To Martin Gardner, for years of encouragement and inspiration

martinGardner

Credits

Cover design by Larry Lurin

Book design and composition
by Marcos Vergara and Scott Kim

Copyright Information

Publishing Information

Published in the United States
by Random House, Inc., New York,
and simultaneously in Canada
by Random House of Canada, Limited.

Manufactured in the United States of America

0 9 8 7 6 5 4 3 2 1

ISBN 0-679-75595-0

New York   Toronto   London   Sydney   Auckland

Trademarks

Contents

* Originally published in *NeXTWORLD* magazine. All other puzzles from *NewMedia* magazine.

Introduction

This book is for puzzle lovers, computer fans, multimedia folk, and anyone who likes to give their mind a workout. Although the puzzles were originally written for computer magazines, none of them require any particular technical knowledge. Everything you need to solve each puzzle is included on the page.

Think of this book as a mental gym. Each chapter exercises a different style of thinking: Sound plunges you into the world of digital audio. Graphics exercises your visual perception. 3-D lets you flex your spatial thinking muscles. Interaction gives you a chance to think about the intricacies of human-computer interaction. Motion challenges your ability to think in time. And finally, Programming gives you a behind-the-scenes look at what makes software tick.

Most of the puzzles in this book were originally published in *NewMedia* magazine. Several are from the now defunct magazine *NeXTWORLD*, which covered the NeXT computer and NeXTSTEP computing environment.

NewMedia Magazine covers the field of multimedia — the emerging combination of the computer, publishing and television industries. Multimedia includes such diverse phenomena as two-way cable, CD-ROM publishing, video games, online networks, interactive books and personal computers.

If ever there was a interdisciplinary field, multimedia is it. Multimedia teams typically include such diverse fields as graphic design, sound recording, cinematography, and computer programming, not to mention writing, game design, and psychology.

The puzzles in this book touch on all the types of thinking that go into multimedia. For those who want to go deeper into each topic, there are additional challenges, background discussions, and suggestions for further reading with each puzzle. If you are a teacher, you may want to use the puzzles to teach computer science, graphic design, computer graphics, or multimedia. In the answers section you will find some responses from readers.

Enjoy your workout. Drink lots of water and let your brain cool down for five minutes between puzzles. And don't be surprised if you learn something in the process.

For a whirlwind tour of multimedia, see *Understanding HyperMedia* by Bob Cotton and Richard Oliver. For practical advice on producing multimedia, see *The Multimedia Bible* by Jeff Burger and *Multimedia Power Tools* by Peter Jerram and Michael Gosney. To read about the value of developing different thinking styles, see *Frames of Mind* by Howard Gardner.

Notes of Thanks

Thanks to my editor at *NewMedia* Gillian Newson for her cheerful support and clever quotes. Thanks to Marcos Vergara for his tireless graphic production and artistic touches. Thanks to Dan Ruby, Eliot Bergson, and the crew at *NeXT-WORLD* for an enjoyable stint as puzzle columnist. Thanks to Ben Calica, the editor at both *NewMedia* and *NeXTWORLD* magazines that originally suggested my puzzle columns. Thanks my editor Mike Roney, production manager Jean Davis Taft, and Niki DiSilvestro at Random House for their support and guidance. And thanks to David Bunnell and the crew of *NewMedia* for making my job so rewarding.

Behind the Scenes

Here are the steps I take when I design a puzzle, using Process of Elimination as an example.

1. Choose a topic. The first NewMedia puzzle, created by editor Ben Calica, was a multiple choice trivia quiz about the multimedia industry. The first NeXTWORLD puzzle, created by editors Dan Ruby and Dan Lavin, was a crossword puzzle that contained many words from NeXT culture. In both cases the editors started with a standard puzzle format, then adapted it to a particular a topic. Crossword puzzles and jigsaw puzzles, by far the most popular types of puzzles, are created this way.

My approach is different: I start with a topic, then find a suitable form. Teachers create exercises for students this way. Of course school exercises can be boring; my challenge is to make puzzles that both teach and entertain.

When I began Process of Elimination, I had just heard about the CD-ROM Making It Macintosh (now published as the *Electronic Guide to Macintosh Human Interface Design*). I learned that the visual design had been done by Lauralee Alben and Jim Faris of Alben & Faris, an established graphic design firm that had recently entered the field of user interface design.

When I visited Alben & Faris I put on my journalist hat, looking for an interesting story angle. The two designers showed me pages of preliminary icons they had sketched for the program MacInTax. I was struck by the quantity and variety of their sketches. So I decided to create a puzzle about the process of icon design.

2. Identify a key skill. Once I had chosen the topic of icon design, my next step was to isolate a particular mental skill that I wanted readers to exercise. Process of Elimination focuses on the skill of critiquing alternative designs. A Matter of Interpretation, which also concerns icon design, focuses on the skill of considering alternate interpretations, while An Eye for an Icon focuses on the skill of making pictures look good at a low resolution

My puzzles focus on skills, like how to critique an icon, rather than facts, like the pixel width of a Windows icon, for four reasons: fact-based puzzles require knowledge that many readers do not have, facts in a fast moving field like computers go out of date quickly, terminology varies from computer to computer, and skills have wider application than facts.

3. Break it into simple pieces. When readers do puzzles they do not just read about a topic, they participate. To make participation easy, a puzzle designer must keep the mechanics simple. The trick is to retain the essential experience while eliminating irrelevant details. For instance, toys like wooden blocks retain the experience of building three-dimensional structures while eliminating the need for manual dexterity.

For Process of Elimination I simplified icon design by giving readers predefined icon sketches and evaluations, eliminating the need for drawing or writing skills. Even though the choices are limited, the puzzle retains the essential experience of looking at icons with a critical eye and weighing alternatives.

4. Choose a form. Process of Elimination takes the form of a matching game: each icon matches exactly one evaluation, and there are the same number of icons as evaluations. Alternatively, I could have chosen a multiple choice format with several possible evaluations for each icon.

I prefer the matching format because it has a natural drama missing in the multiple choice format. Every time the reader makes a match, the pool of potential matches shrinks. If the reader makes a wrong match at some point, then later in the game the reader will get stuck with matches that don't make sense and will know to back up. In contrast, multiple choice tests give the reader no feedback as to whether the answers are right. Finally, there is a pleasing sense of closure when all matches are complete.

The matching format lets me address many different issues at once, from purely graphic criticisms to considerations of meaning. I used a similar format for the puzzle You Call the Shots, which covers an equally wide range of issues. In contrast, the puzzle Look on the Bright Side, which uses a ranking format, looks at only one issue: the brightness of an image.

Puzzles that use a matching form are easy to grade—an important consideration for a contest that can sometimes receives thousands of entries. I always include at least one worked-out example, so readers are sure they are writing answers in the correct form.

5. Compose the Puzzle. Once I had figured out the general architecture of Process of Elimination, I had to fill in the details. First I decided which icons to use. Then I wrote the evaluations, making sure that there was only one possible right answer. Finally I put the evaluations in a random order.

Different types of puzzles pose different compositional problems. To compose You Call the Shots I studied the movie *It's a Wonderful Life* in detail to find a single sequence that included many types of shots. To compose mathematical puzzles like Once a Pong a Time or Go Non-Linear I exhaustively checked out all possibilities to see if there were alternate solutions. For Lost in HyperText I first composed the solution, then added extra paths while being careful not to introduce alternate solutions. I wrote computer programs to help me compose Format Maze and Get with the Program. I commissioned Larry Kay to write the story for A Likely Story.

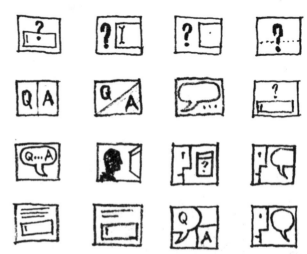

6. Test It and Tune A good puzzle should be hard enough to be challenging, but not so hard that it is discouraging.

The only way to tell for sure how well a puzzle works is to test it on other people. A puzzle that seems easy to me often turns out to be too hard for other people.

In the first draft of Process of Elimination, the twenty evaluations were divided into five sets of four evaluations each. Each of the first four icons went with one from the first four evaluations, each of the second set of four icons went with one from the second set of four evaluations, and so on. Since the reader only had to match four icons at a time, this version turned out to be too easy.

To make the puzzle harder I merged all the evaluations into a single list, so that any of icon might go with any of the twenty evaluations. I also had to rewrite a couple of the evaluations to fit the new form.

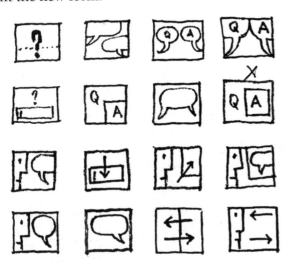

Alben & Faris

7. Add Finishing Touches. The final step is to dress up the puzzle with an interesting presentation. First I chose the title Process of Elimination. Then my editor Gillian Newson added the quotation and put it in Greek letters just for fun. Finally graphic artist Marcos Vergara added the gray screens behind the icons to add visual interest and make the groupings clearer. If I had been designing a computer game instead of a paper game, I would have also added animation and sound.

I often have the final presentation in mind when I begin a puzzle. When I saw Alben & Faris's sketches I imagined how intriguing a page full of icon sketches would look. Once I had chosen the actual icons, Jim Faris redrew the sketches so they would go together better.

Puzzle makers often wrap their puzzles in fictional settings that motivate the peculiar circumstances of the puzzle. I added brief fictional settings to Who's in Front? and The Scarlet Letter, but usually I find that the real-life story provides plenty of motivation.

The purpose of a skill-based puzzle like Process of Elimination is to let you experience a particular style of thinking. The answer gives you a goal to work toward, and a way of checking your progress, but is not an end in itself. The important thing is what happens to your mind in the process. I want you to leave Process of Elimination seeing the world a bit differently from when you began. Perhaps you will find yourself looking at an icon one day and wonder how it might have been designed differently.

CHAPTER 1

Sound

The puzzles in this chapter exercise some of the basic skills of a musician or audio engineer—the ability to translate sounds into musical notation, sound waves, and other visual representations.

Watching the Months Roll By, The Third Wave, and Parts of Speech look at sound as sound waves. Lip Sync looks at speech in terms of the mouth positions of an animated character. Music to My Eyes challenges you to read music in a player-piano roll notation. Format Maze takes you into the all too common nightmare of converting media from one format to another. Sounds Like lets you sample the fascinating world of sound effect artists.

To increase your awareness of sound, take a moment to sit quietly and listen to the sounds in your environment. List everything you can hear. What is the most distant sound? What is the quietest sound? Can you hear voices? Can you hear sounds within your own body? Turn your head. How do the sounds change? Now stand up as quietly as you can. How many different sounds do you hear as you stand up?

Filmmakers have known for years that sound is a powerful way of grabbing people's emotions. Animators and documentary filmmakers often plan their soundtracks first, then cut the picture to match the sound.

Now multimedia producers are learning about the importance of good sound. Sound in multimedia not only includes music, but also sound effects, voice, ambient sound, and audible feedback from user actions like pressing a button. Multimedia sound artists must combine the skills of a musician, recording engineer, sound effect artist and user interface designer.

Video games have always had sound, but except for a few beeps most software has been silent. As computers merge with cable television and stereo systems, we can expect future multimedia productions to feature more sophisticated uses of sound.

Four key innovations make multimedia audio practical: digital audio, which represents sound with perfect fidelity in number form; MIDI, which represents musical information in a compact but flexible form; compact disks and other optical media, which store the large amounts of data needed for digital audio; and signal processing chips, which put a recording studio in your personal computer.

To learn more about the physics and psychology of hearing, see *The Science of Musical Sound* by John Pierce. To learn more about the world of MIDI and digital audio, see *MIDI for the Professional* by Tim Tully and Paul Lehrman, and *Principles of Digital Audio* by Ken Pohlmann.

Watching the Months Roll By

Computers store sounds as waves. People who work with sound waves, like recording engineers and computer musicians, learn to look at a sound wave and imagine approximately how it sounds.

For instance, shown below is the sound wave for the phrase "computer graphics." Notice that short choppy regions correspond to percussive consonants like hard C, P, or T. Regularly repeating waves correspond to prolonged vowels, like O or U, or prolonged consonants like M or R. Thin irregular waves correspond to hissing sounds, like PH or S.

Shown at right are the sound waves for the names of the twelve months. Can you match each month with its sound wave? For instance, you can see that the three swells of sound wave A correspond to the three syllables of the month November. Write your answers in the blanks.

Answers on page 107.

Ever wonder what a sound looks like?

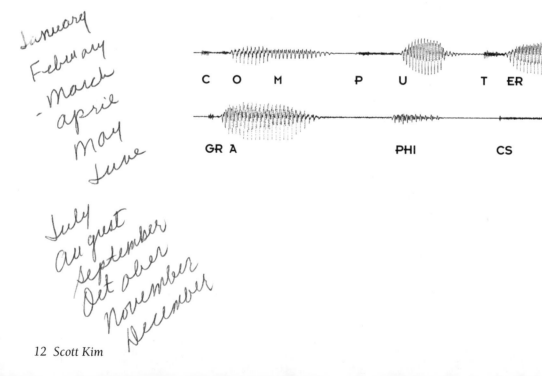

C O M   P U   T ER

GR A   PHI   CS

January
February
- March
- april
May
June

July
august
September
October
November
December

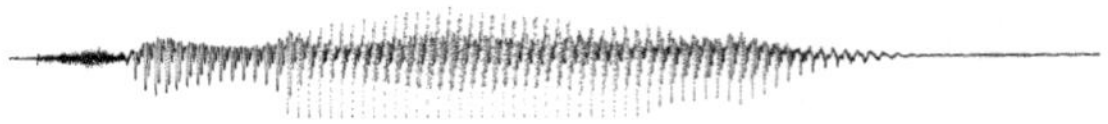

1 _____

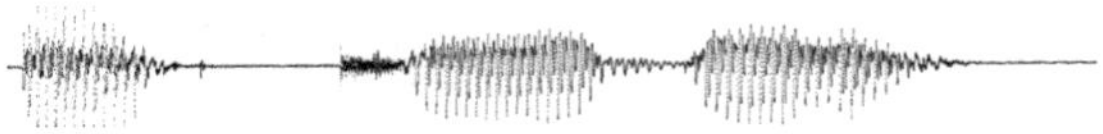

2 _____

3 *August* _____

4 _____

5 *March* _____

6 *May* _____

7 *December* _____

8 _____

9 *June* _____

10 *September* _____

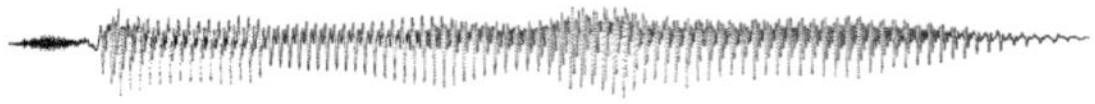

11 _____

12 *November* _____

Parts of Speech

"Give it an understanding, but no tongue" —Hamlet

Some day we will be able to talk to computers instead of typing on keyboards. To make this possible, scientists will have to solve some very hard problems. This puzzle will give you a taste of the difficulties in recognizing words from their sound waves.

Below are the sound waves for 26 different phonemes. Notice that vowels like A and O and open consonants like L and M are periodic waves; sharp consonants like K and P are sudden spikes; and sibilants like S and SH are random waves. Waves for M and N are very similar.

At right, I have written a dozen slightly altered proverbs, using sound waves in place of key words.

Each sound wave is spliced together from several phonemes. The missing words turn the proverbs into sayings about multimedia. For instance, Proverb 1 is "All that glitters is not Hollywood," and is made up of the phonemes Hat-pOt-Lake-scEne-hOOt-gOOd-Day.

Can you fill in all the missing words? Write your answers in the blanks provided. Each blank is a single word. By the way, real voice recognition is much harder than this puzzle—the breaks between phonemes are not so distinct.

Hint: The sound for long I as in mIne is made of two sounds, O as in pOt and E as in scEne. Answers on page 107.

mAn	Ate	Boy	Day	Scene	bEd

Get	Hat	pIn	Kite	Lake	My	Nice

pOt	vOte	hOOt	gOOd	Put	Rag

Song	SHe	Ten	THis	Ud	Very	Zone

1. All that glitters is not _____ Hollywood _____.

2. The pen is mightier than the _____.

3. Look before you _____ *click* _____.

4. Haste makes _____.

5. The grass is greener on the other _____.

6. Brevity is the soul of _____.

7. When in _____, do as the Romans.

8. _____ can't be choosers.

9. Don't count your chickens before they _____.

10. Better _____ _____ than sorry.

11. Familiarity breeds _____.

The Third Wave

$$i\hbar\frac{\partial\psi}{\partial t} = \frac{-\hbar^2}{2m}\nabla^2\psi + V\psi$$

—Erwin Schrödinger

Compact disks and other digital media store sounds as numbers that describe sound waves. Shown below are brief excerpts of two sound waves. Notice that the first wave oscillates twice in the time it takes for the second wave to oscillate once. That's because the first tone is higher in pitch, and the waves for higher pitches oscillate faster.

When two tones sound at once, the numbers in the waves add. I have added the two waves below to make a third composite wave. If you were to play this wave through a speaker you would hear both of the original tones at the same time. Notice that the two component waves reinforce each other at the first peak (1+1=2), and cancel each other at the second peak (1–1=0).

At right I have taken six simple sound waves and added them up two or three at a time to make new waves. Can you identify which waves I added? We've given you the first answer. Write your answers in the blanks below, one letter per blank. Answers on page 107.

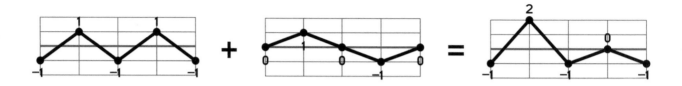

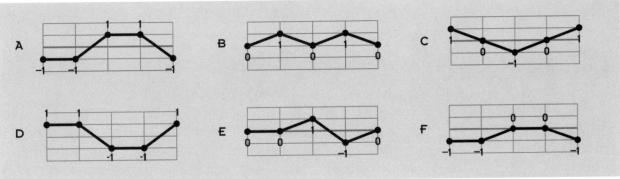

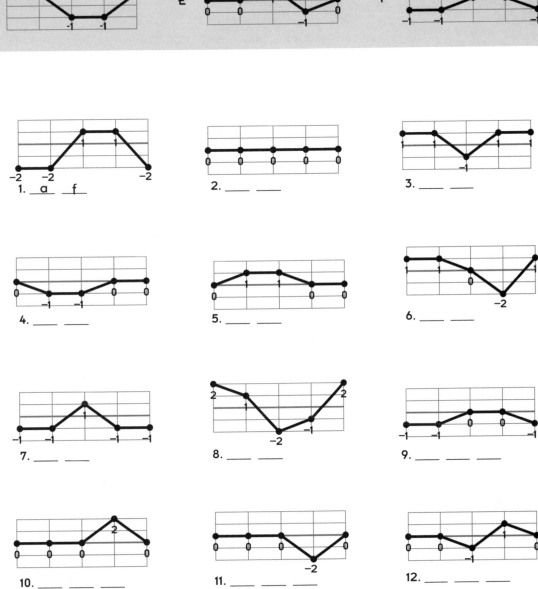

1. __a__ __f__

2. ____ ____

3. ____ ____

4. ____ ____

5. ____ ____

6. ____ ____

7. ____ ____

8. ____ ____

9. ____ ____

10. ____ ____ ____

11. ____ ____

12. ____ ____

Lip Sync

Everybody will be making faces in the mirror to solve this puzzle— don't forget to enunciate.

Talking heads—close-up shots of people speaking—are a common visual device in movies and television. As computers become household appliances, talking heads are becoming a common device on computer screens.

Speech is much easier to understand and—especially if the face of the speaker is visible—more expressive. But full-motion video of talking heads takes large amounts of storage, and is limited to a fixed number of phrases.

To solve this problem, Bright Star Technology has developed HyperAnimation, a technology that animates speaking faces from a small number of mouth positions, much the way animators have animated speech for years. For instance, the top row shows the mouth positions for the phrase "numbers game." Notice that a single letter sometimes requires two mouth positions (A), and that one mouth position sometimes stands for two different sounds (M and B).

The groups labeled A through J show the mouth positions for the numbers one to ten. Can you match the mouth positions with the numbers? Once you have solved the numbers, try reading the well-known, three-word phrase at the bottom of the page.

Hint: watch your mouth in a mirror and speak the words slowly. Try exaggerating your mouth movements. Answers on page 107.

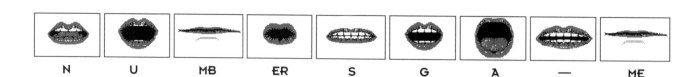

N   U   MB   ER   S   G   A   —   ME

1. _____

2. _____

3. _____

4. _____

5. _____

6. _____

7. _____

8. _____

9. _____

10._____

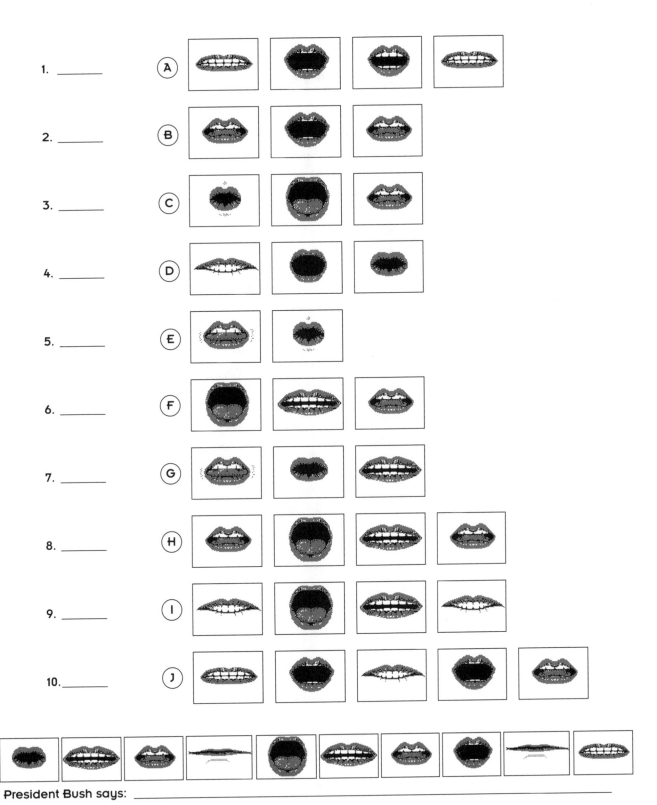

President Bush says: _____

Music to My Eyes

"Music is feeling, then, not sound."
—Wallace Stevens

MIDI—Musical Instrument Digital Interface—has revolutionized the way that music is composed and performed in much the same way that digital audio has revolutionized the way music is recorded. MIDI is a standard compact communications protocol that lets keyboards, synthesizers, and software from different manufacturers all talk the same language without sacrificing quality or flexibility. Without MIDI the world of electronic music would suffer the same fate as the tower of Babel.

Much of the music you hear these days is composed with MIDI-based sequencer programs like Passport Designs' MasterTracks or Opcode's Vision. Like a multitrack tape recorder, a sequencer lets you edit and mix many different instruments, each in its own track. For instance, the score at right shows 12 instruments playing simultaneously. Each shade of gray is a different track, and each horizontal bar is a separate note. Time moves to the right, and higher pitches are higher on the page.

A sequencer represents sound as a series of notes, not as a continuous sound wave. That means you can change the pitch or duration of a note after it has been recorded by dragging its bar in the score, or even change which instrument plays on which track.

In the score at right, each track represents a different children's song. For instance, the black melody G in the middle is "Frère Jacques." Notice how the melody starts by going up twice and then back down, then repeats itself. The 11th note is held longer, so its bar is twice as long. Even if you don't read music notation, you can still see the shapes of these melodies.

Below the score is a list of song titles. Can you match each song with its track? The songs have been transposed into different keys to avoid collisions.

Hint: Try whistling each melody and notice whether each note goes up or down from the previous note.

Thanks to Paul Lehrman of Music and Technology in Boston for suggesting the idea for this puzzle. Lehrman is co-author, with Tim Tully, of *MIDI for the Professional*, published by Amsco Publications. Answers on page 107.

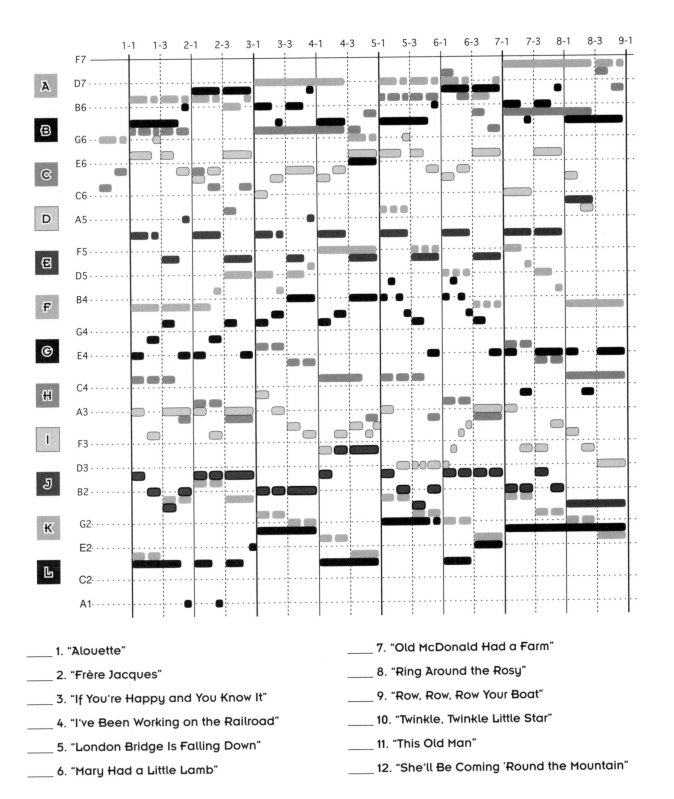

_____ 1. "Alouette"

_____ 2. "Frère Jacques"

_____ 3. "If You're Happy and You Know It"

_____ 4. "I've Been Working on the Railroad"

_____ 5. "London Bridge Is Falling Down"

_____ 6. "Mary Had a Little Lamb"

_____ 7. "Old McDonald Had a Farm"

_____ 8. "Ring Around the Rosy"

_____ 9. "Row, Row, Row Your Boat"

_____ 10. "Twinkle, Twinkle Little Star"

_____ 11. "This Old Man"

_____ 12. "She'll Be Coming 'Round the Mountain"

Format Maze

"A mighty maze! but not without a plan."
—Alexander Pope

Whether it is converting a digital sound from one file format to another, transferring a videotape from Hi-8 to VHS, or translating English to Japanese, getting things into the right form can be like running a maze. Every time a new format comes out the problem gets worse, because it must be backwards compatible with previous formats.

You start with a file in a format that works on one computer that you want to move to another computer. However, the other computer won't read your disk, so you use a disk conversion program. But the conversion program doesn't recognize your file format, so you use yet another program to convert the file to a different format. But can you reach the final format? Good luck!

Here's a format conversion maze to try just for fun. Start from the document labeled E which is saved in the current document format. Your goal is to convert the document into each of the other nine target document formats by moving along the lines from computer to computer.

Every time your file reaches a computer, you must convert the file using one of the conversions listed on the screen. If no conversion applies, then you are stuck.

Under each of the target documents write the minimum number of conversions it takes to get there. For instance, you can get to document G in three conversions: 1) E>J, 10) J>I, 11) I>G. No document takes more than 12 conversions. Answers on page 108.

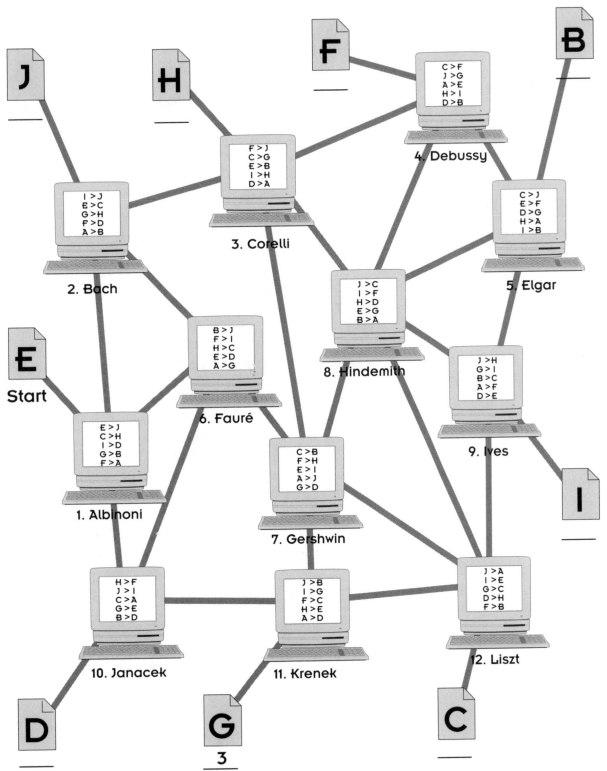

J

H

F

B

C > F
J > G
A > E
H > I
D > B
4. Debussy

I > J
E > C
G > H
F > D
A > B
2. Bach

F > J
C > G
E > B
I > H
D > A
3. Corelli

C > J
E > F
D > G
H > A
I > B
5. Elgar

E
Start

B > J
F > I
H > C
E > D
A > G
6. Fauré

J > C
I > F
H > D
E > G
B > A
8. Hindemith

J > H
G > I
B > C
A > F
D > E
9. Ives

E > J
C > H
I > D
G > B
F > A
1. Albinoni

C > B
F > H
E > I
A > J
G > D
7. Gershwin

I

H > F
J > I
C > A
G > E
B > D
10. Janacek

J > B
I > G
F > C
H > E
A > D
11. Krenek

J > A
I > E
G > C
D > H
F > B
12. Liszt

D

G
3

C

Sounds Like

"Was that cannon fire, or was it my heart pounding?"
—Casablanca

Sound effects have a long history: theater, radio, movies, television and now multimedia. In the 1950s, a film editor at Universal Pictures named Jack Foley came up with the idea of assembling a studio where he could perform and create live sound effects for movies. The name stuck, and now live sound-effects performers are called Foley artists. They are also called Foley walkers because one of the most common sound effects is foot-steps—almost every footstep you hear on television was created by a Foley walker.

Foley artists need a good sense of timing, so it comes as no surprise that many have backgrounds in dance. In the past 15 years the number of professional Foley artists has grown enormously. Look for them in movie credits.

Most sound effects are straight-forward—a door sounds like a door, handcuffs sound like hand-cuffs—but some are less obvious. Sometimes substitutes are more convincing than the original—the real sound of a fist hitting a face is not very dramatic—so directors and sound designers re-create sounds in the studio to make them more vivid. The sound of the train at the beginning of *Tombstone*, for example, was created entirely with objects recorded in a studio.

Science-fiction movies, especially, require resourceful thinking. The sound of the laser blasts in *Star Wars* was created by hitting a tension wire supporting an antenna with a hammer, then processing the sound in a studio.

Veteran Foley artist Allison Moore helped me assemble this list of sound effects and their sources. Can you match each effect with its source? Write your answers in the blanks. Answers on page 108.

EFFECT

- **F** 1. Block of ice sliding on floor
- ___ 2. Bone crushing
- ___ 3. Body stabbing
- ___ 4. Horse hooves
- ___ 5. Brain surgery
- ___ 6. Dog collar jangling
- ___ 7. Clothes rubbing against self
- ___ 8. Walking on snow
- ___ 9. Rubber gloves
- ___ 10. Car suspension
- ___ 11. Boat at dock
- ___ 12. Fire
- ___ 13. Ice cubes clinking
- ___ 14. Person sitting in car seat
- ___ 15. Walking on leaves
- ___ 16. Bicycle
- ___ 17. Walking on grass

SOURCE

- A. Balloon
- B. Pen caps floating in glass
- C. Luggage cart
- D. Creaky floor
- E. Knife in watermelon
- F. Bowling ball on floor
- G. Newspaper being crunched up
- H. Squeaky chair
- I. Wet chamois cloth
- J. Celery
- K. Set of keys
- L. Leather purse
- M. Pillowcase
- N. Coconut shells
- O. Walking on grass mat
- P. Walking on cornstarch
- Q. Walking on 1/4-inch recording tape

CHAPTER 2
Graphics

The puzzles in this chapter exercise some of the basic skills of an artist or graphic designer—the ability to think critically about the purely visual aspects of an image.

RGB Mixup, Out of Proportion, Counter Proposal, and Look on the Bright Side look at the perception of color, proportion, negative space and brightness, and are similar to exercises given in basic art classes. Filter Fantasies and Worf Morph explore ways that computers can transform images. Package Deal encourages you to look critically at product packaging.

To heighten your visual awareness, look at your surroundings and try some of these games: Look only for things that are red. How many circular things can you see? Imagine how they would look if they were square. Find two things that are the same shape but have completely different functions. What is the largest rectangle you can see?

Early computers communicated by printing characters on rolls of paper. Today's computers communicate in detailed full-color imagery, animation, and three-dimensional modeling.

Graphics in multimedia include not just images, but also text, diagrammatic graphics, animation, movies, and on-screen controls like buttons. An important difference between television and interactive media is that images do not have to be recorded in advance, but can be synthesized in response to the user's actions.

Multimedia graphic designers come from a number of different backgrounds. Each background has its liabilities. Fine artists need to learn how to make images that communicate technical ideas. Graphic designers need to learn to think in time. Animators and 3-D artists need to learn to handle text. And user interface designers need to learn basic art skills.

To learn more about graphic design, see *Problems: Solutions* by Richard Wilde and *Envisioning Information* by Edward Tufte. To enhance your ability to see like an artist, see *Drawing on the Right Side of the Brain* by Betty Edwards, *Experiences in Visual Thinking* by Robert McKim, and the CD-ROM *VizAbility* by Gayle Curtis, Scott Kim, and Kristina Hooper Woolsey.

Counter Proposal

When we read words, we rarely notice the shapes of the letters. To a graphic designer or multimedia designer, however, letters are important visual elements. The shape of an initial capital letter or the texture of a paragraph can influence the look of a screen every bit as much as the color of a button or the brightness of an illustration can.

One of the more important visual aspects of a letter is not the letter itself but the space around the letter, also called negative space. For instance, the W that begins this article has three enclosed or partially enclosed spaces, called counters, and two other negative spaces before and after the letter.

Below are 26 counters or other negative shapes from the typeface Minion. Each shape comes from a different capital letter. For instance, shape 15 comes from the letter W. Can you match each shape with the corresponding letter shown below? Some shapes can match more than one letter, but there is only one way to match every shape with a different letter.

Hint: Shapes are all in the right orientations, and are all the same size. Answers on page 108.

> "The hardest thing to imagine is the space between the stars."
> —A. Herbert

A B C D E F G H I J K L M

— — — — — — — — — — — — —

N O P Q R S T U V W X Y Z

— — — — — — — — — — 15 — — —

Look on the Bright Side

O ne of the basic properties of an image is its overall brightness, also called its lightness, value, luminance, or intensity. Even if some areas of a picture are black, the average brightness can be quite high if the black areas are balanced by large areas of white. For instance, image A at right has an overall average brightness of 6 percent on a scale from 0 percent (black) to 100 percent (white).

Years of writing on paper has trained us to think of images as black lines on white paper. Computer screens imitate the appearance of paper with screens that are mostly white. Such images are extremely bright, especially when the image is illuminated. That's why titles for luminous media like slides, movies, and multimedia productions often favor light letters on dark backgrounds. (Light backgrounds are still best for large amounts of text.)

Brightness is especially important to consider when you cut from one image to another. Typically, the overall brightness of a movie stays about the same within a scene, even when the camera cuts from one angle to another. Big changes in brightness tend to occur at scene changes. Similarly, major brightness changes in a multimedia production are best used at major transitions.

Can you rank the images at right from lightest (largest percentage of white pixels) to darkest? Write your answers in the blanks below. Answers on page 109.

"Dark with excessive bright."
—Paradise Lost

1.____ 2.____ 3.____ 4.____ 5.____ 6.____ 7.____ 8.____ 9.____ 10.____ 11.____ 12.____

A

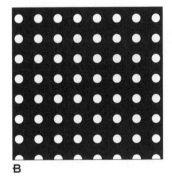

B

C

D

E

F

G

H

I

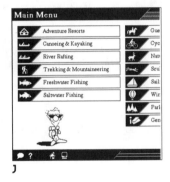

J

K

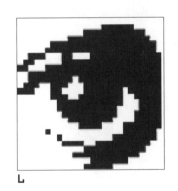

L

Out of Proportion

There's more than one way to squash a masterpiece.

Televisions, books, stationery, movies, and computers all come in rectangles of familiar proportions. For instance, American letter paper is a rather squat 8.5 by 11 inches, while German paper is a slimmer 210mm by 297mm. The difference is slight, but to someone accustomed to seeing one format, the other format looks unusual.

Movies have always tended toward wider formats. The standard 640 by 480 pixel computer screen is in the same 4:3 proportion as a television screen, which was in turn based on the proportions of early movies. The new high-definition television format has a wider 16:9 format that approximates the wide screen dimensions of today's movies, which are almost twice as wide as they are tall. Cinerama, the widest format of all, was nearly three times as wide as it was tall.

When wide screen movies are transferred to conventional video-tape, which displays a 4:3 rectangle, they are sometimes "letterboxed" to preserve the original proportions. Even though letterboxing actually makes the picture smaller by blacking out the top and bottom areas of the screen, the effect is to make the screen look larger. In general, wide screen formats look more expansive because the eye sees a wider angle horizontally than vertically.

Here are twelve rectangular images stretched to be in the wrong proportions. Can you match each of the 12 images with its proper shape among the black rectangles? No two are the same proportion. Answers on page 108.

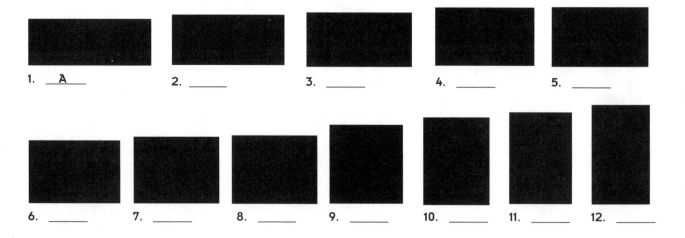

1. __A__   2. _____   3. _____   4. _____   5. _____

6. _____   7. _____   8. _____   9. _____   10. _____   11. _____   12. _____

A. Cinerama

B. Diskette

C. Dollar Bill

D. American Stationery

E. German Stationery

F. License Plate

G. HDTV

H. Business Card (wide)

I. Paperback Book

J. CD Case

K. Slide

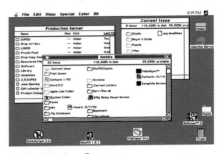

L. Computer Screen

RGB Mixup

"To paint well is simply this: to put the right color in the right place" —Paul Klee

If you look very closely at a television screen or color computer monitor you will see that the picture is made of red, green, and blue dots or vertical bars.

Every color under the sun can be made by combining different amounts of these three light-based primary colors, because the cones in the backs of our eyes perceive color by detecting different amounts of red, green, or blue light. Theatrical lights also come in red, green, and blue. If you turn on all three colors you see white light.

Shown below are examples of what happens when you mix up the cables for the red, green, and blue channels on a computer monitor.

The first picture shows all three channels plugged in correctly. Pictures 2–4 show only one channel at a time, while pictures 5–7 show two channels at a time.

Can you label the channels for the remaining pictures? Hint: Pretend the three boxes below each picture are three plugs on the back of your monitor and that writing a letter in a box represents plugging a cable from your computer into your monitor.

For example, picture 8 shows what happens when you put the green cable in the red plug, and the red cable in the green plug. Write your answers in the blanks. Answers on page 108.

Original

Red channel

Green channel

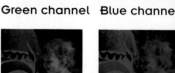

Blue channel

Red+Green

Red+Blue

Green+Blue

8	Red	Green	Blue
	G	R	B

9	Red	Green	Blue

10	Red	Green	Blue

11	Red	Green	Blue

12	Red	Green	Blue

Filter Fantasies

"Shootout at the Fantasy Factory" —Traffic

Image editing programs like Adobe Photoshop, Aldus PhotoStyler, and Electronic Arts' DeluxePaint let you transform a simple piece of black and white artwork into a full-color fantasy in a few simple steps—and you don't have to draw a thing.

Instead of drawing, you use filters, which operate on an entire image at once. Digital filters go far beyond their photographic counterparts. Not only can they color and blur images, they can bend them into spirals, explode them into clouds and colorize them in ways that an airbrush can't touch.

Below are six effects I created using Kai's Power Tools (labeled A-F). By combining different effects in different orders I created the six images at right (numbered 1–6) from the same original art. For instance, image No. 1 was created using filter C, then filter A. You can tell that A came after C because the shadow from A blurs the blue halo from C.

Can you figure out which effects I used and in what order I applied them to create the other five images? No effect is used twice in the same image. Write your answers in the blanks. Answers on page 109.

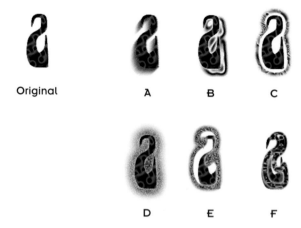

Original   A   B   C

D   E   F

Original

1.   <u>C</u>   <u>A</u>   <u>   </u>

2. <u>   </u> <u>   </u> <u>   </u>

3. <u>   </u> <u>   </u> <u>   </u>

4. <u>   </u> <u>   </u> <u>   </u>

5. <u>   </u> <u>   </u> <u>   </u>

6. <u>   </u> <u>   </u> <u>   </u>

Worf Morph

How do you turn a man into a woman? If you're in the special effects business, the answer is "morphing," a technique for gradually transforming one image into another.

The simplest way to combine two images is to superimpose them with a dissolve or double exposure. Unfortunately this works only if the all the features are in exactly the same positions in both pictures.

To do better, programs such as Morph by Gryphon Software let you pick out corresponding points in the two images, such as the center of the eye or the edge of the mouth. Once you have specified matching points, the software warps the two images until the features align.

Then it does a simple dissolve to produce a composite image. Morphs work best when the source images have similar camera angle, lighting, and background.

Morphing is regularly used to show transformations of the character Odo in the television show *Star Trek: Deep Space Nine*. Shown below are the faces of ten characters from the television programs *Star Trek: The Next Generation* and *Star Trek: Deep Space Nine*. I used the program Morph to combine pairs of faces. For instance, Morph 1 combines the faces of Picard and Sisko H and I. The last three morphs each combine three faces. Can you identify which faces were combined in each morph? Answers on page 110.

> "God hath given you one face and you make yourselves another."
> —Hamlet

A. Michael Dorn as Worf

B. Terry Farrell as Dax

C. Armin Shimerman as Quark

D. Brent Spiner as Data

E. Marina Sirtis as Troi

F. Rene Auberjonois as Odo

G. Colm Meany as O'Brien

H. Patrick Stewart as Picard

I. Avery Brooks as Sisko

J. Nana Visitor as Kira

1. __H__ __I__

2. ____ ____

3. ____ ____

4. ____ ____

5. ____ ____

6. ____ ____

7. ____ ____

8. ____ ____

9. ____ ____

10. ____ ____ ____

11. ____ ____ ____

12. ____ ____ ____

Package Deal

A good package design has a clear visual identity, even if you see only a corner of the box. Here are twelve CD-ROM package covers, plus two close-ups from each cover.

Can you identify from which package each close-up came? For instance, close-up 1 comes from the distinctive orange border of Just Grandma and Me.

Answers on page 110.

Pack • ag • ing n. The act, process, industry, art or style of packing

A. B. C. D.

E. F. G. H.

I. J. K. L.

1. __A__   2. ____   3. ____   4. ____   5. ____   6. ____   7. ____   8. ____

9. ____   10. ____   11. ____   12. ____   13. ____   14. ____   15. ____   16. ____

17. ____   18. ____   19. ____   20. ____   21. ____   22. ____   23. ____   24. ____

CHAPTER 3

Motion

The puzzles in this chapter exercise some of the basic skills of an animator, or filmmaker —the ability to imagine how objects move and change over time.

Who's In Front?, In Transition, and Going Around in Cycles touch on basic concepts in animation. You Call the Shots gives you a chance to think as a filmmaker telling a story. Around the Rainbow, Get in the Swing, and Halfway Olympics look at some of the ways computers can be used in animation.

To step into the shoes of an animator, imagine getting up and walking across the room. Which part of your body do you move first? Where do your feet touch the ground? If you attached a light to the top of your head, what path would it trace? At any given time, what part of your body is moving most quickly?

Motion has always been closely associated with life—the word animation comes from the Latin word *anima*, meaning life. Motion attracts attention—the most basic use of animation in computers is the blinking cursor, which calls attention to where your typing will appear. Motion improves apparent picture quality—television is able to get away with crude picture quality compared with print because the picture moves.

Motion in multimedia includes prerecorded video, visual transitions from one screen to another, pre-drawn animated elements, and synthesized three-dimensional models. Computers and video games are currently struggling to achieve the same fluidity of motion that television and movies have had for years.

To learn more about animation and the language of film, see *The Animation Book* by Kit Laybourne, *The Critical Eye* by Margo A. Kasdan and Christine Saxton, and *Thinking in Pictures* by John Sayles.

In Transition

Multimedia producers know all their transition effects, so pan right and iris open on this puzzle.

Transitions have been a common part of the filmmaker's visual vocabulary for many years. Now they are part of the multimedia producer's vocabulary.

Shown below are six ways to animate a transition from one scene to another using NewTek's Video Toaster. I've combined three to five different transitions in each of the images at right. To produce the first image, for instance, I combined the trees and flowers with a Blocks transition (D). Then I added some of the fish with a Wipe (A) stopping a little less than halfway across. Finally I dropped in the face with a Trajectory transition (F).

Note that Swap and Trajectory shrink the image. Swap exchanges the left and right halves. Images can be frozen at any point during a transition.

For each image at right, can you list the transitions in the order they were applied? The source images are shown at the top of the page. No transition is used more than once in the same image. Check your answers on page 110.

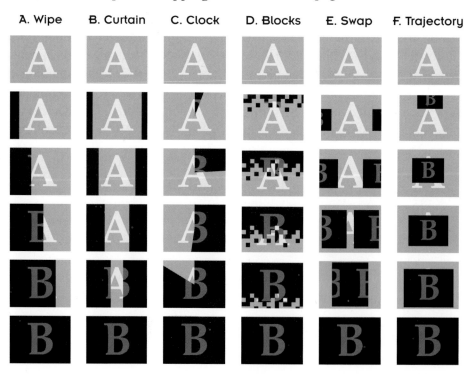

A. Wipe B. Curtain C. Clock D. Blocks E. Swap F. Trajectory

1. <u>D</u> <u>A</u> <u>F</u>

2. ___ ___ ___

3. ___ ___ ___

4. ___ ___ ___ ___

5. ___ ___ ___ ___

6. ___ ___ ___ ___ ___

Who's In Front?

It may not look too difficult, but these stampeding letters could give you a headache. It's easier (and more fun!) with a partner.

At right are four frames of an animation created with the multimedia authoring program MacroMedia Director. Each letter is in a separate plane stacked from front to back like sheets of transparent paper. Animators call these planes "cels." The cels are stacked in the same order in all four frames. Can you list the letters in order from front to back?

To solve the puzzle, look carefully to see which letters pass in front of which other letters. For instance, you can see that F is in the front-most plane because no other letter passes in front of it. You might think that O is the next letter because O is behind F in frame one. But in frame two F passes in front of R and in frame three R passes in front of O, so R comes between F and O.

Hint: X comes somewhere in front of W and the backmost letter is V. Answers on page 110.

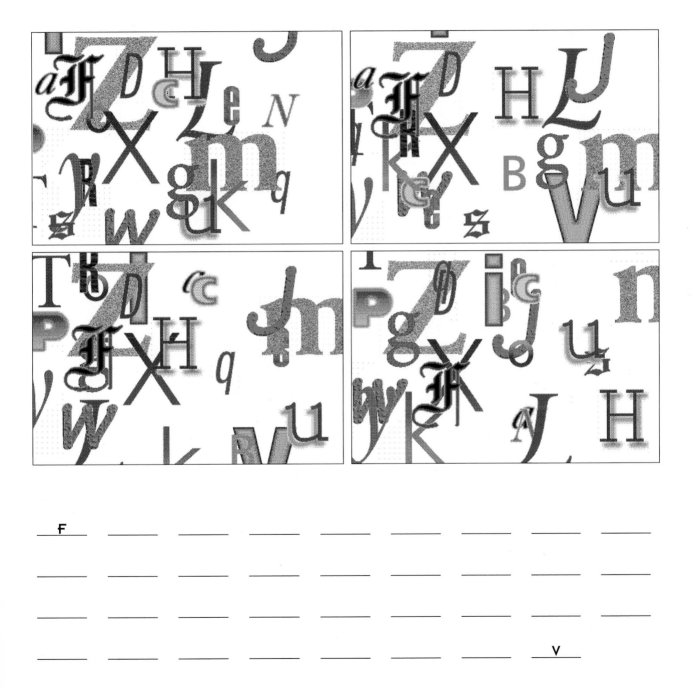

F _____ _____ _____ _____ _____

_____ _____ _____ _____ _____

_____ _____ _____ _____ _____

_____ _____ _____ _____ V _____

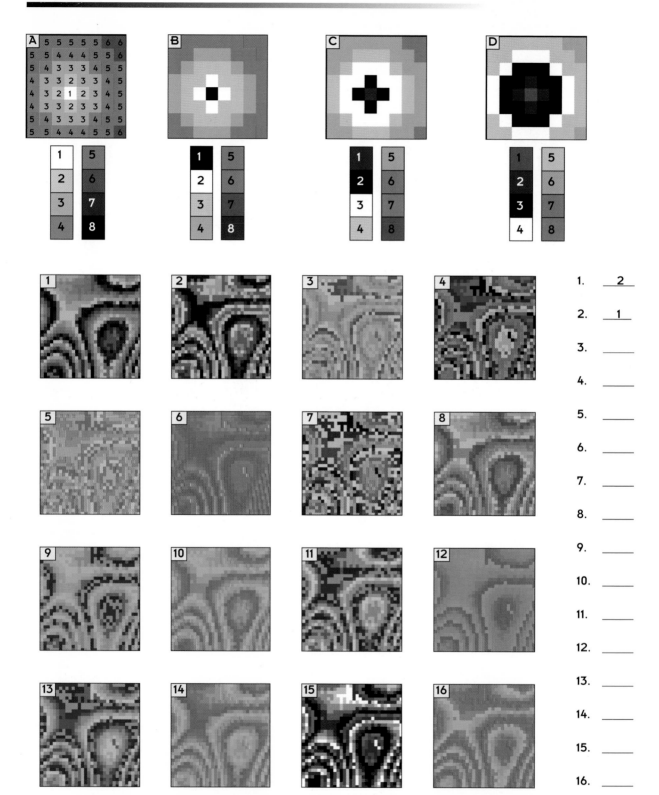

Around the Rainbow

First there was op art, then black lights and lasers. Now color cycling is the latest way to blow your mind with graphics. This programming trick adds animated flowing colors to a static image, creating a big effect with a little programming.

Screen savers such as NuTopia's Flow Phazer use color cycling to create psychedelic effects. Artist Mark Ferrari used Electronic Arts Deluxe Paint's color cycling features to animate daylight shifts for the software Seize the Day. Synergy and TECNATION DIGITAL WORLD use color cycling software to create hypnotic light shows for dance clubs and musical performances.

You can create your own color cycles using tools like Macromedia Director. Example A at left shows an image and its color table. Each pixel in the image gets the number of a slot in the color table: For instance, the center pixel gets 1 and the upper-right pixel gets 6.

If you change a color in the color table, all pixels with the matching number change to that color: For instance, if you change Slot 3 to black, all pixels with color 3 turn black, as in Example D. Note that

colors 7 and 8 appear in the color table but not in this image.

Examples B, C, and D show what happens when color cycling is turned on. In Example B the color in Slot 1 moves to Slot 2, Slot 2 moves to Slot 3, and so on. Slot 8 moves to Slot 1. The same thing happens from Example B to C and from C to D. After eight steps, the cycle repeats. Color cycling looks best when the colors form a smooth progression.

Sixteen copies of the same image with different color tables are shown at left. These color tables have 16 slots each, but only colors 1 through 10 appear in the image. Can you match pairs of images that have the same color table but different cycling? For instance, Image 2 has the same table as Image 1, cycled by three slots. Some images match more than one other image individually, but there is only one way to pair up all images at the same time.

Hint: look for images that contain bands of similar colors. Images 10 and 14 contain the same colors but in opposite order, so are not part of the same cycle.

Synergy created the images for this puzzle. Answers on page 110.

"And all the colors I am inside have not been invented yet."
—Shel Silverstein

Get in the Swing

"It don't mean a thing if it ain't got that swing." —Irving Mills

If you want to create an animation with realistic human motion, there is no better source than the human body. Disney's first animated feature, *Snow White*, is a good example. To animate the title character, the moviemakers filmed a live actress, then traced over the movie a frame at a time with a technique called rotoscoping.

Rotoscoping captures two-dimensional motion. The computer-modeled characters that appear in today's movies and multimedia productions require three-dimensional motion data.

To meet this need, companies like BioVision have developed three-dimensional motion capture systems. Here's how it works: The pictures in the first column at right show San Francisco Giants manager Dusty Baker at bat. Reflective markers are strapped to his head, elbows, bat, and other key points. Six video cameras shoot the motion at 200 frames per second from six different points of view.

A computer operator uses proprietary software to compute 3-D coordinates for each reflective marker. The data can be displayed many ways: as dots in space, from different points of view, as a stick figure, or as any other 3-D model. BioVision Motion Data has been used in medicine, sports, movies, and video games.

Frames A through F are in order. The other three rows are not. For instance, Image 1 matches Frame F. Can you match each image with the correct frame? Hint: The video and the dots are not from the exact same frames. Check your answers on page 110.

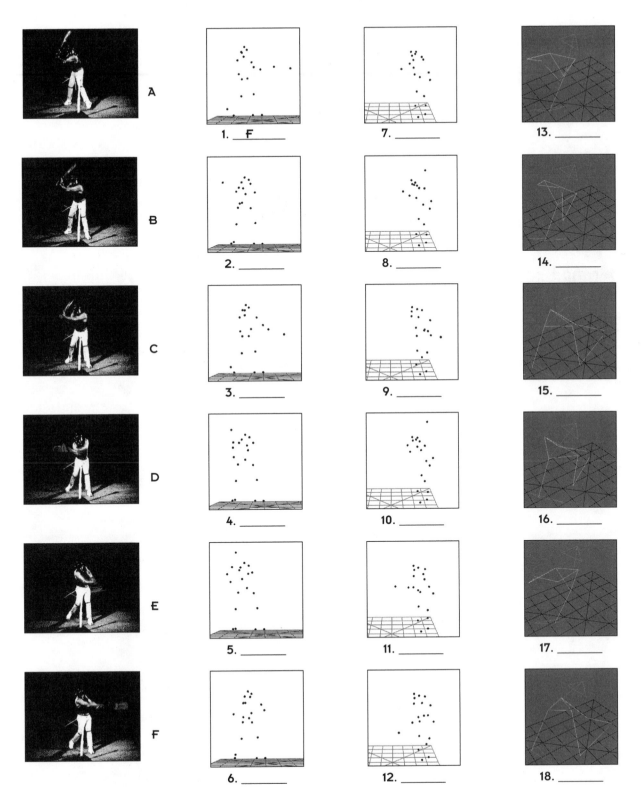

1. __F__

2. _____

3. _____

4. _____

5. _____

6. _____

7. _____

8. _____

9. _____

10. _____

11. _____

12. _____

13. _____

14. _____

15. _____

16. _____

17. _____

18. _____

Going Around in Cycles

"And go 'round
and 'round and
'round . . ."
—Joni Mitchell

Animators are forever repeating themselves. Consider the man running around the bottom of this page, created in Cinemation, an animation program published by Vividus. After six frames he returns to the beginning position. Such a repeating sequence is called a cycle.

To draw this cycle, the animator had to imagine how the different masses of the body shift and bounce. Note that the head bobs up and down, the body tilts forward and back, and the limbs get longer and shorter.

Repeat the cycle and you can make the character run forever. Of course, real people do not move exactly the same way with every step. Saturday-morning cartoons with limited budgets use cycles extensively, whereas animated films of theatrical quality use different drawings for each movement.

At right are six animations. I've given you the first frame of each cycle. Can you put the remaining five frames of each cycle in order? Hint: the bird extends its wings forward and out on the downstroke. Write your answers in the blanks.

The bird and cantering horse were photographed by Eadweard Muybridge in the 1870s. The bird's upstroke is twice as fast as its downstroke. The donkey was modeled in Playmation by Anjon & Associates. Luxo Jr. (not a complete cycle) was animated by John Lasseter and Tom Porter of Pixar. The pivoting Charles Barkley (not a complete cycle) from Colossal Pictures, is by Mike Smith, Richard Quan, and David Wise. The steaming cereal was drawn by Lynda Weinman. Answers on page 110.

E   A

1. <u>A</u> <u>B</u> <u>C</u>
   <u>D</u> <u>E</u>

D   B

C

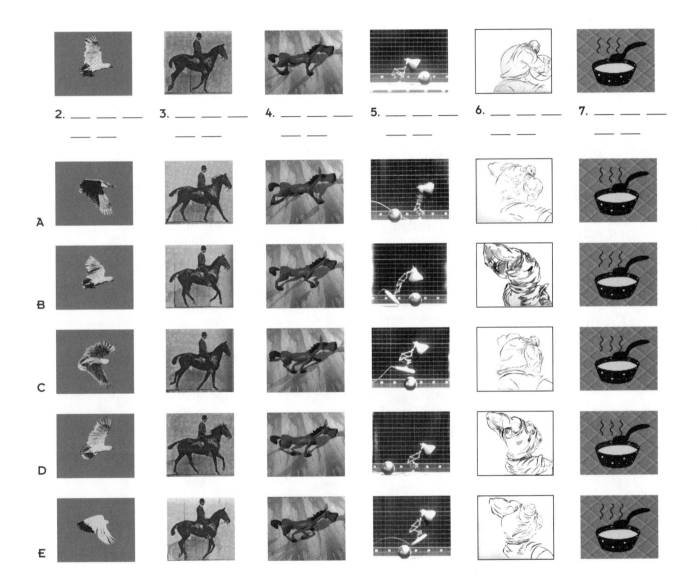

2. ___ ___ ___
___ ___

3. ___ ___ ___
___ ___

4. ___ ___ ___
___ ___

5. ___ ___ ___
___ ___

6. ___ ___ ___
___ ___

7. ___ ___ ___
___ ___

A

B

C

D

E

You Call the Shots

Good directors put meaning into every camera angle. Find the subtle messages Frank Capra laced into this classic movie.

Early multimedia productions were largely sequences of static images which used the visual conventions of books and magazines. As the industry matures, multimedia productions are beginning to use the visual conventions of movies and video.

One of the most important elements of movie composition is the way camera angle and distance are used to show relationships among characters. For instance, notice that the shots at right, taken from a scene in the movie *It's a Wonderful Life,* progress from long to close, mirroring the increasing emotional intensity of the scene.

Long shots, in which the camera is far enough away to see actors from head to toe, emphasize settings. Close shots frame the actor's face from the shoulders up, emphasizing facial expression. Medium shots end approximately at the actor's thighs. Over the shoulder shots show how actors relate to each other in space.

Diagonal shots tend to be more dynamic. Shots from above—high angle shots—tend to make actors appear small and overpowered, while low angle shots tend to make actors appear large and overpowering. Panning shots turn the camera from side to side to follow the action, while tilt shots aim the camera up and down. Shots in which the camera moves are called tracking shots—or crane shots when the motion is vertical. Tracking shots give a more vivid sense of motion than zoom shots, in which the camera stays still.

Here are twelve shots, plus the types of shots and their purposes. Can you identify the type and purpose of each shot? Each type and purpose is used just once. Answers on page 110.

1. _____

2. _____

3. ___L R___

4. _____

5. _____

6. _____

7. _____

8. _____

9. _____

10. _____

11. _____

12. _____

TYPES OF SHOTS:

A. Close
B. Tracking close
C. Medium close
D. Medium low
E. Long
F. Low angle
G. Over the shoulder
H. Over the shoulder close
I Over the shoulder low angle
J. Medium diagonal
K. Medium (slightly high)
L. Over the shoulder high angle

PURPOSE:

M. Character is in an overseeing role
N. Shows reaction of character
O. Characters reach a resolution
P. Character is a vivid presence
Q. Near character dominates
R. Far character is small and childish
S. Character on right is higher, more aggressive

T. Characters react to previous shot
U. Framing emphasizes character on right
V. Framing emphasizes a nervous hand
W. Establishes spatial relationship of characters
X. Character is engulfed by flowers

Halfway Olympics

In a traditional animation studio one artist draws the key frames (every tenth frame or so) and other more junior animators draw the in-between frames. Many people have tried to automate in-betweening with computers. Unfortunately automated in-betweening tends to lack the fluid life that an animator can breathe into a line drawing.

Despite its limitations, computer in-betweening has found a useful place in the world of special effects, especially when the movements are not intended to look natural. For instance, the illustration program Adobe Illustrator includes a tool called Blend that draws the stages between two given shapes. Shown below is a five-stage blend.

Shown at right are ten symbols from the 1972 Summer Olympic Games, and twelve blended symbols. Note that I omitted pieces of equipment such as the soccer ball in Soccer and the bicycle in Cycling. Each blended symbol is exactly halfway between two of the original Olympic symbols.

Can you figure out which pairs of symbols are blended? For instance, event 1 is halfway between symbols B and D. Write your answers in the blanks. You might also enjoy giving names to the composite sports events. Answers on page 110.

> "Some people are so fond of ill-luck that they run half-way to meet it."
> —Douglas Jerrold

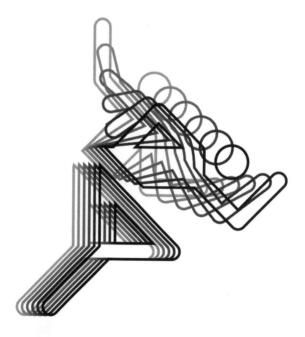

A. Gymnastics   B. Track & Field   C. Boxing   D. Fencing   E. Swimming

F. Volleyball   G. Basketball   H. Soccer   I. Wall-contact Sports   J. Cycling

1. **B   D**

2. ___ ___

3. ___ ___

4. ___ ___

5. ___ ___

6. ___ ___

7. ___ ___

8. ___ ___

9. ___ ___

10. ___ ___

11. ___ ___

12. ___ ___

CHAPTER 4
Interaction

The puzzles in this chapter exercise some of the basic skills of a human factors engineer or human-computer interaction designer—designing products that people can use easily, safely and effectively.

A Likely Story lets you experience the challenge of writing for interactive media. A Matter of Interpretation, Process of Elimination, and An Eye for an Icon unravel the process of designing symbols that communicate clearly. The Scarlet Letter and The State of the Button take you inside the workings of on-screen controls. Once a Pong a Time pays tribute to the video game that foreshadowed interactive multimedia.

To think like an interaction designer, watch people using a photocopying machine. What errors do users make? How does the machine foil user expectations? How could you redesign the machine to reduce errors? How does the machine show the user what it can do? How does the machine give feedback to the user that an operation has been successfully completed?

The field of human factors was started during World War II because engineers found that if they did not place controls consistently then airplane pilots might end up ejecting themselves when they meant to land. Similarly, engineers designing nuclear power plants did not want operators to accidentally press the wrong button. Human factors engineers often have backgrounds in psychology, and understand the importance of testing designs on potential users.

Interaction is what makes computers and other interactive media different from television. Television is a passive medium that gives the viewer no control other than to change channels. At the very least, interactive media give the viewer the ability to choose different paths through the sea of information. Beyond simple choice, interactive media can also allow viewers to play with interactive simulations, create their own content with software tools, and communicate with other people via electronic mail.

To learn more about interaction design and human engineering, see *The Art of Human-Computer Interaction Design* edited by Brenda Laurel, *The Design of Everyday Things* by Don Norman, the journal *Interactions,* and game designer Chris Crawford's journal *Interactive Entertainment Design.* You can read more about icon design in *The Icon Book* by Willliam Horton.

A Likely Story

In conventional fiction, the writer crafts a sequence of events that leads to an inevitable conclusion. The reader has no choice but to follow the set story line. The challenge for the writer is to plan the sequence so events unfold naturally yet serve the drama of the story.

In interactive media, the reader can follow different branches of the story tree. There may be many paths through the story, even multiple conclusions. The challenge for the writer is to plan a web of events that lets the reader explore freely yet always have a coherent experience.

The diagram below shows the structure of a branching story. Arrows show all the possible paths through the story. Node 1 is the first paragraph, and nodes 12 and 13 are the two possible endings.

At right are the thirteen paragraphs of the story in scrambled order. Can you assign a part to each node so that every path story path makes sense? Write your answers in the blanks below. For instance, the answer to 1 is A, and node 1 must be able to be followed by node 2 or node 3. You might enjoy trying to write your own branching story to fit the diagram.

Larry Kay, author of Freddi Fish from Humongous Entertainment, is a multimedia writer and game designer specializing in animated adventure comedy entertainment and family-oriented edutainment. Answers on Page 111.

> "The life of every man is a diary in which he means to write one story, and writes another."
>
> —Sir J. M. Barrie

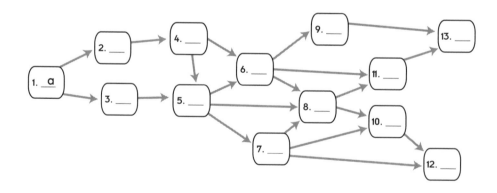

Bob Barley and Patty Droog are aging rock stars who have always had a tempestuous relationship. Bob, the songwriter, has always had trouble controlling his thirst for liquor. Patty, the lead vocalist, has always had trouble controlling her thirst for young men. They've been apart for the last two years, but the're about to meet again in…

The Rise and ¿Fall/Rise? of Virtual Sponge

©1994 by Larry Kay

A. Upon the urging of friends, Bob and Patty form the band "Virtual Sponge."

B. Virtual Sponge plays a high school prom. Patty flirts with all the young dudes. Bob and a teacher get drunk.

C. Bob picks a fight with Patty's young hunk and beats him mercilessly. Patty calls the police. Virtual Sponge is history.

D. Skinny Marv, the influential club owner of Fat's, tells Bob and Patty that he wants to be the first to put Virtual Sponge on the map.

E. Lulu Funnstock, an excellent rep from Wild Cherry Records senses magic in the performance. She makes quick contact and is ready with a nice recording contract.

F. Bob, despondent at his lack of self-control, needs to be alone. Months go by. Bob is now penniless, but he has written new songs and has new self-control. He performs on the street.

G. Oprah Winfrey hosts a TV show, "Rock Bands That Split Up," and her guests are Virtual Sponge. They perform a song without rehearsal, and it comes off quite all right.

H. Bob gets some small gigs with his new material. One night, Patty is in the audience. Bob calls her up on stage for a few numbers. They talk about recording together.

I. Bob is furious when he is handcuffed and taken to jail.

J. Virtual Sponge plays to a packed house at Fat's. Bob's performance is off because he got drunk. Patty is furious.

K. Sleazoid producer, Harry "The Hose" Hummer, steps from the shadows, whispers to Bob, and takes him in a limo to a private party where there's plenty of booze, hookers, and drugs. Bob thinks he spots a couple of undercover vice squad cops, but The Hose tells him not to be paranoid.

L. Bob passes out, drunk. He revives as Patty is about to leave with a young hunk. Bob makes a scene, yelling that he and Patty are finished. That's fine with Patty.

M. The recording session is going badly. When Patty enters you could cut the tension with a knife. Finally, Bob asks her to sing on his new ballad. Their duet becomes a hit single.

A Matter of Interpretation

"Of shoes—and ships—and sealing wax—of cabbages—and kings"
—Lewis Carroll

Icons were invented in 1975 by David Canfield Smith at the Xerox Palo Alto Research Center to make computers easier to work with. Today, computer screens feature the familiar file folder and the document with a folded corner, first drawn by graphic designer Norm Cox as part of the Xerox Star computer system. Icons often used in multimedia productions include the play, rewind, and pause icons common on stereos and VCRs.

Why use icons instead of words? Here are five reasons: They attract attention. They are memorable. They usually take less space on the screen. They usually have the same meaning for people who speak different languages. And they give people a familiar spatial sense of what they are doing.

But icons can be ambiguous. Is icon "a" the noun "eye," the verb "look," or the adjective "visible"? Or does it stand for a more general idea like "sensory" or "body part"? The problem gets worse when you try to invent icons for ideas that are difficult to picture, like "create" or "find." So before decorating your next multimedia production with icons, ask yourself whether words would be clearer.

At right are 16 icons and 16 pairs of words. Each icon can be interpreted in at least two ways. Your challenge is to place each of the icons in the middle of one of the pairs to form two common two-word phrases or compound words. Many of the answers involve puns. For instance, icon A makes both the phrase "private eye" and the compound word "sea (see) horse." Be sure to write both the letter for the icon and the two meanings. Answers on page 111.

A. (eye symbol)   I. (pointing hand symbol)

B. (sun symbol)   J. (car symbol)

C. (waves symbol)   K. (duck symbol)

D. (envelope symbol)   L. (snowflake symbol)

E. (rose symbol)   M. (watch symbol)

F. (footprints symbol)   N. (bell symbol)

G. (palm tree symbol)   O. (pencil symbol)

H. (match symbol)   P. (spray can symbol)

1. private ___eye___ ___A___ ___see___ horse

2. family _____ _____ _____ reader

3. birth _____ _____ _____ out

4. pig _____ _____ _____ handed

5. grand _____ _____ _____ dog

6. cold _____ _____ _____ seed

7. head _____ _____ _____ job

8. may _____ _____ _____ hips

9. hand _____ _____ _____ side

10. rapid _____ _____ _____ box

11. chain _____ _____ _____ head

12. half _____ _____ _____ word

13. ocean _____ _____ _____ opener

14. street _____ _____ _____ graph

15. board _____ _____ _____ charming

16. white _____ _____ _____ saw

Process of Elimination

Ιχον: Φρομ τηε Γρεεκ εικον, αν ιμαγε ορ σψμβολ τηατ ρεπρεσεντσ α σπεχιφιχ χομμανδ

Like dressing for a special occasion or choosing a name for a baby, designing a good icon is a search for perfection. A graphic interface designer may reject dozens of alternatives before finding one that satisfies all the design criteria. Shown at right are sketches by interface designers Alben & Faris that led to five icons for Chipsoft's tax preparation program MacInTax. In each row there are four sketches, three that were eliminated and one that led to the final solution.

Each icon illustrates a different design challenge: "Electronic Filing" shows how changing the position of elements can change its meaning; "Open Forms" icons draw on computer conventions; "Interview" shows ways an icon can be misinterpreted; "Tax Summary" represents different degrees of abstraction; and "Filing Cabinet" shows how even the simplest icon can have many different graphic variations.

To the right of the icon sketches is a list of evaluations. Can you match each icon with its evaluation? Each evaluation is used just once. Sometimes an icon may have more than one plausible evaluation; pick the one that seems most relevant and write your answers in the blanks. Answers on page 111.

ICONS

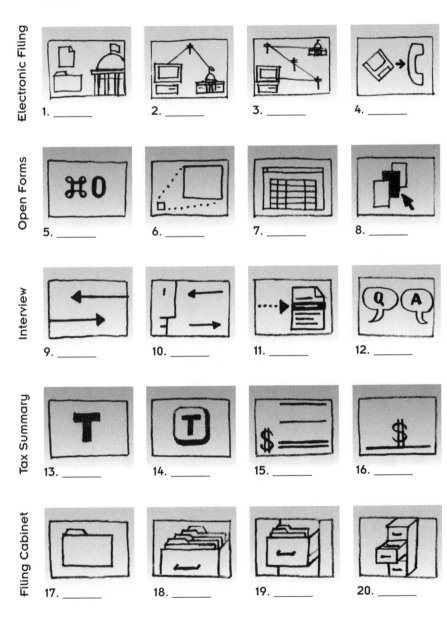

Electronic Filing

1. _____ 2. _____ 3. _____ 4. _____

Open Forms

5. _____ 6. _____ 7. _____ 8. _____

Interview

9. _____ 10. _____ 11. _____ 12. _____

Tax Summary

13. _____ 14. _____ 15. _____ 16. _____

Filing Cabinet

17. _____ 18. _____ 19. _____ 20. _____

EVALUATIONS

A. No: Too far.

B. No: Too close.

C. No: A floppy wants to talk on the telephone.

D. No: Lacks a cabinet.

E. No: Something is going two ways, but what?

F. No: Party, shirt or time out?

G. No: Animation of an icon opening into a window.

H. No: The bottom line, literally.

I. No: Does not show that the documents are moving.

J. No: Makes you think of William Tell.

K. No: Is there a scale model of a building on your desk?

L. No: Might not see it's a calculator key.

M. No: Only if you are familiar with keyboard commands.

N. No: An open window, not a list of forms.

O. No: Only if you know the look of the official IRS forms arrow and menu selection.

P. Yes: Two lines means "total" to an accountant.

Q. Yes: Select one of many forms.

R. Yes: Ask a question, get an answer.

S. Yes: Just the right distance.

T. Yes: From the computer, over telephone lines, to the government, far away.

An Eye for an Icon

Icon designers are masters of detail. Here are fifteen NEXTSTEP icons; all except the Lotus Improv icon were designed by NeXT interface designer Keith Ohlfs. Each icon was drawn in 48 by 48 pixels with just four colors: black, white, light gray, and dark gray. (In current versions of NEXTSTEP, icons are in color.)

Look carefully and you'll see a high degree of detail in these low-resolution icons. The details often become unrecognizable when you look at them close up. For instance, the address on the envelope in icon A turns out to be the speckled pattern in close-up 1.

Each of the remaining close-ups matches part of one of the icons. No two close-ups match the same icon. All close-ups are right-side up and enlarged by a factor of 400 percent. Can you match each close-up with its icon?

Answers on page 112.

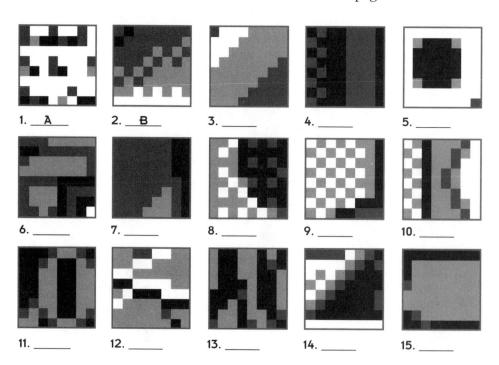

1. __A__ 2. __B__ 3. _____ 4. _____ 5. _____
6. _____ 7. _____ 8. _____ 9. _____ 10. _____
11. _____ 12. _____ 13. _____ 14. _____ 15. _____

"Our life is frittered away by detail . . . Simplify, simplify." —Henry David Thoreau

A.

B.

C.

D.

E.

F.

G.

H.

I.

J.

K.

L.

M.

N.

O.

The Scarlet Letter

Creating the graphical user interface for a piece of software can be an arduous process. Fortunately, current software development environments such as InterfaceBuilder for NeXTSTEP and Visual Basic for Windows let you create the look of a program simply by dragging premade interface elements from a palette. For instance, one of the InterfaceBuilder palettes is shown below.

I used InterfaceBuilder to create a custom application called The Scarlet Letter. There are six controls, each with two positions: horizontal slider (left or right), vertical slider (top or bottom), radio buttons (the white button is the one selected), button (turns white when pressed), switch (checked or unchecked), and pop-up list (one of two possible words).

Each control affects a different variable, each with two values: background color (light gray or medium gray), foreground color (dark gray or black), letter (A or B), case (upper or lower), style (regular or italic), and orientation (right side up or upside down).

Unfortunately some prankster has changed all the labels on my controls. All I was able to salvage were these four screen shots. Can you figure out which variable is affected by which control? Write the values of the variables in the blanks at right. For instance, liberal might be dark gray and conservative might be black. Check your answers on page 112.

> "Who controls the past controls the future: who controls the present controls the past."
> —George Orwell

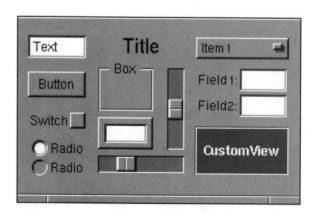

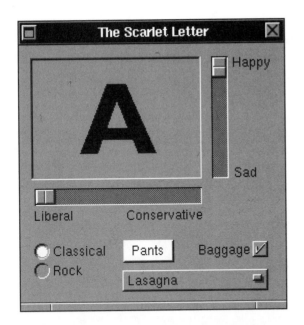

Liberal _____ _____ Conservative

Happy _____ _____ Sad

Classical _____ _____ Rock

Pants (pressed) _____ _____ Pants (not pressed

Baggage (checked) _____ _____ Baggaged (not checked)

Lasagna _____ _____ Ravioli

The State of the Button

The check box is one of the simplest user interface elements. Click to turn it on, click again to turn it off—just like a light switch. Behind the apparent simplicity, however, lurk many subtle design issues common to all button interactions.

Below is a history of a check box interaction. In Step 1, the user gets ready. In Step 2, the user moves the cursor into the check box but has not yet pressed the mouse button, so the box does not change.

The user presses the mouse button down in Step 3, causing the edge of the box to be highlighted by getting thicker. This feedback tells the user that the button has been clicked but not yet checked.

In Steps 4 and 5, the user keeps the mouse button held down and moves the cursor out of the check box and then back in, causing the box to unhighlight then rehigh-

light. In Step 6, the user releases the mouse button, causing the box to unhighlight and become checked.

Below the anchovy example is a summary of the interaction. To its right is a table describing all possible states of the check box. The rows list all possible user actions, and the columns list all possible check box states. Tables like this one are often used by electrical engineers to analyze digital circuits.

For each possible current state, the table tells you what the next state will be for a given user action. For instance, cell 1 in row 1 tells you that when the check box is unhighlighted and unchecked, mouse down will cause the check box to highlight.

Blank cells represent impossible combinations. For instance, cell 2 in row 1 is empty because when the check box is already highlighted the user cannot mouse down, because the mouse is already down.

"On Fortune's cap we are not the very button."
—Guildenstern in Hamlet

1. ▲☐ Anchovies

2. ☐ Anchovies

3. MOUSE DOWN! ☐ Anchovies

4. ▲☐ Anchovies

5. ☐ Anchovies

6. MOUSE UP! ⊠ Anchovies

☐ Down ☐ Leave ☐ Enter ☐ Up ⊠

ACTION	PREVIOUS STATE			
	☐	☐	⊠	⊠
Mouse Down	☐		⊠	
Mouse Enter	☐		⊠	
Mouse Leave		☐		⊠
Mouse Up	☐	⊠	⊠	☐

Here are nine interaction sequences, with their first and last states, and nine state transition tables. For each sequence, can you find a table that transforms the first state into the last state? For instance, the first sequence matches Table A. Some sequences can match more than one table, but in the final answer each sequence matches a different table. Answers on page 112.

A 1. □ Down Leave Enter Up ☒

___ 2. ■ Down Up Down ☒

___ 3. ☒ Down Leave Up ☒

___ 4. ☒ Down Leave Enter Leave ■

___ 5. □ Down Up Down Leave □

___ 6. ■ Down Up Down Up □

___ 7. ☒ Down Leave Enter Leave Enter ■

___ 8. ☒ Down Leave Enter Leave Up ☒

___ 9. □ Down Up Down Up Down ☒

A.

	□	□	☒	☒
Down	□	□	☒	☒
Enter	□	□	☒	☒
Leave	□	□	☒	☒
Up	□	☒	☒	□

B.

	□	□	☒	☒
Down	□	□	☒	☒
Enter	□	□	☒	☒
Leave	□	□	☒	☒
Up	□	□	☒	☒

C.

	□	□	☒	☒
Down	□	□	☒	☒
Enter	□	□	☒	☒
Leave	☒	☒	□	□
Up	☒	☒	□	□

D.

	□	□	☒	☒
Down	□	□	☒	☒
Enter	□	□	☒	☒
Leave	□	□	☒	☒
Up	□	□	☒	☒

E.

	□	□	☒	☒
Down	□	□	□	□
Enter	□	□	□	□
Leave	☒	☒	☒	☒
Up	☒	☒	☒	☒

F.

	□	□	☒	☒
Down	□	□	☒	☒
Enter	□	☒	☒	□
Leave	☒	☒	□	□
Up	☒	□	□	☒

G.

	□	□	☒	☒
Down	☒	□	☒	□
Enter	□	☒	☒	□
Leave	□	□	☒	□
Up	☒	☒	☒	☒

H.

	□	□	☒	☒
Down	□	□	☒	☒
Enter	☒	□	□	☒
Leave	☒	☒	□	□
Up	□	☒	☒	□

I.

	□	□	☒	☒
Down	□	□	□	□
Enter	□	□	□	□
Leave	□	□	□	□
Up	□	□	□	□

Once a Pong a Time

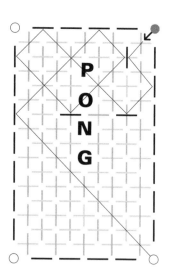

When you strip away all the fancy graphics and sound, the essence of interactive multimedia is interaction. Nothing illustrates this better than the first hit video game, Pong, masterminded by Nolan Bushnell in 1972.

Pong is a version of ping-pong in which two players maneuver paddles to bounce an electronic blip back and forth across the screen. The graphics and sound are simple, but the interactive experience is so good that people will play it for hours. When the first Pong machine had been installed for a week, the machine stopped working. The problem? The coin box was jammed full of quarters.

Multimedia producers can learn much from video games. Here are four principles of video game design well illustrated by Pong:

Immediate involvement: No installation, no manuals, no screens full of menus; Pong invites you to start playing and learn as you go.

Immediate feedback: Turn the knob and the paddle moves, hit the ball and you hear a beep, win a round and your score increases.

Uninterrupted rhythm: Computer-based multimedia productions often pause awkwardly

during disk accesses or long computations; video games never make the user wait.

Simulated behavior: By reproducing the physics of a bouncing ball, Pong gives the player complete freedom to bounce the ball in any direction, not just along a few predetermined paths.

This puzzle pays tribute to Pong. A ball is released from the upper right corner of a playing field. When it hits a wall or bumper, it bounces off like a pool ball and changes direction. When it hits a white circle it stops. When it hits a letter, it keeps going in a straight line. For instance, the ball in the example at left follows the path shown, bouncing nine times as it passes over P and O, then ending at a white circle.

Can you place just three bumpers in the field at right so the ball passes over the letters P, O, N, and G in that order? The ball may not pass over any letter more than once before it passes over G.

Draw your answer by darkening three of the pale lines. Count the bounces before the letter G and write the number in the box. For experts only: Can you get 12 or more bounces? Answer on page 112.

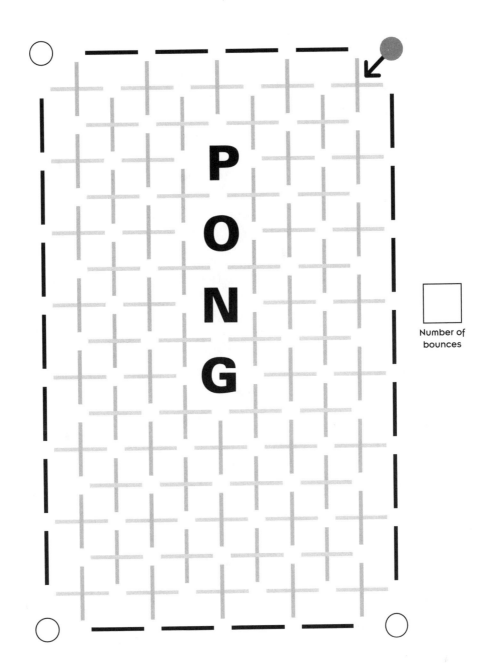

P O N G

Number of
bounces

CHAPTER 5
3-D

The puzzles in this chapter exercise some of the basic skills of a sculptor, architect or engineer—the ability to think in three dimensions.

In-Depth Study takes you into the fascinating world of stereographic imagery. Me and My Shadow, Mental Blocks, and Point of View challenge you to rotate objects in your imagination. Revolutionary Thinking and What a Relief! are based on some of the transformations common to three-dimensional modeling programs. Coordinated Effort challenges you to think in three-dimensional coordinates.

To deepen your experience of spatial thinking, imagine that the room you are in was turned upside down and you were walking on the ceiling. Where would you need to step over a barrier? Where would you need to duck? Now imagine that you are six inches tall. How would you get from the floor to the top of a table, shelf, or other surface? Now imagine that your hand is ten feet long. Imagine reaching into the room and running your hands over things in the room. Where are the large open spaces? Where are the tight spots?

We live in a 3-D world, but until recently all our communication media, like books and movies, have been 2-D. Only those people who work with inherently three-dimensional material, like sculptors, architects, and chemists, usually go to the trouble of building 3-D models. Now 3-D computer graphics lets us build, modify, and move around 3-D models with the same ease that word processors help us write. Important uses of 3-D computer graphics include computer-aided design for automobiles, stereographic imaging for modeling organic molecules, and special effects for movies.

The technical innovation that makes 3-D computer graphics possible is computer chips for synthesizing 3-D images, pioneered by companies like Silicon Graphics. Versions of these chips are now common in video game machines. In the next few years we can expect 3-D graphics to become a standard part of personal computers and online networks.

To learn more about 3-D computer graphics, see *Introduction to Computer Graphics* by Foley and Van Dam. To enhance your spatial thinking, see the Dale Seymour Publications catalog.

In-Depth Study

Stereographic imagery has been with us since the beginning of photography. Now low-cost hardware and software is bringing the magic of stereo to personal computers, video, and multimedia. The principle of stereography is simple: the left and right eyes see slightly different images, which the brain fuses into a single 3-D scene.

You can fuse the pair of images at right by crossing your eyes: Look at the page to the right straight on. Place a finger six inches in front of the big dot at right. With your eyes focused on your finger tip, move your finger toward and away from the page till you see two dots and three arrows in the background.

Concentrate on the middle arrow until it comes into focus. Then look at the word DEPTH. Each letter should appear further away than the previous. Have

patience; this often takes many minutes to see for the first time. About 10% of the population does not see stereo at all.

Each image below makes a stereo pair with the image to its right. For instance, if you cross your eyes so images A and B merge, you will see the letter T floating just in front of the page. There are twenty three letters in all, five in each row and three if you turn this page ninety degrees counterclockwise and read images A, G, M, S with your eyes crossed.

Can you read the letters and insert blanks to spell an appropriate six-word sentence? Write your answer in the blank. By the way, you can make your own stereographic images with the program Stereolusions or by using the 3-D Stereo Noise feature in Kai's Power Tools. Answers on page 113.

"Be careful, or your eyes might stay that way."
—A Parent

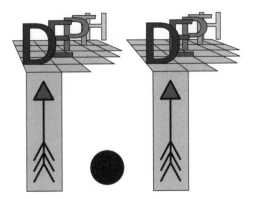

Answer: _____

Coordinated Effort

If you want to design three-dimensional computer graphics, it helps if you can think in three-dimensional coordinates. Solid modeling programs such as Macromedia Macromodel describe objects in terms of numerical coordinates. Each point gets three coordinates that describe its position along three perpendicular directions called the x, y and z axes, similar to the way places on earth can be located by three numbers that describe longitude, latitude and elevation. The coordinates for a point are written in the form (x,y,z).

Shown below are a chair, a table, and a door. Below each picture is a set of coordinates that describes how to draw it. The arrow means to draw a line from one point to another.

> ## "I'm not going to rearrange the furniture on the deck of the Titanic."
> ### —Roger Morton
> #### President Ford's campaign manager

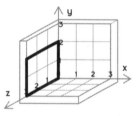

Door
0,0,0➔0,0,3➔0,2,3➔
0,2,0➔0,0,0

Door 1
Add 2 to Y

Door 2
Multiply Z by 2/3, add 1
Multiply Y by 4, add 5
Add 10 to X

Door 3
Exchange X and Y
Add 6 to X
Add 15 to Y

Door 4
Exchange X and Y
Multiply Z by 2/3, add 1
Multiply X by 2, add 1

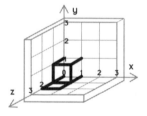

Table
0,0,0➔0,0,1
1,0,0➔1,0,1
1,1,0➔1,1,1
0,1,0➔0,1,1
0,0,1➔1,0,1➔1,1,1➔
0,1,1➔0,0,1

Table 1
Multiply Z by 2
Multiply X by 3, add 3
Multiply Y by 5, add 6

Table 2
Multiply Z by 2
Add 9 to X
Add 14 to Y

Table 3
Add 5 to X
Add 13 to Y

Table 4
Multiply Z by 3
Multiply X by 4, add 6

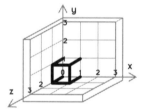

Chair
0,0,0➔0,0,2➔1,0,2➔1,0,0
0,0,1➔1,0,1➔1,1,1➔0,1,1➔0,0,1
0,1,0➔0,1,1
1,1,0➔1,1,1

Chair 1
Exchange X and Y
Multiply Y by 4, add 6
Add 1 to X

Chair 2
Multiply Z by 2
Multiply Y by -1, add 3
Add 6 to X

Chair 3
Multiply Z by 2
Multiply Y by -1, add 3
Add 8 to X

Chair 4
Exchange X and Y
Add 13 to Y
Multiply X by 3, add 1

The place where the three axes cross each other is called the origin, and has coordinates (0,0,0). Coordinates on the x axis get higher going to the right, while coordinates on the y axis get higher going up. Different programs treat the z coordinate differently; in this puzzle z coordinates get bigger as they come toward you.

Below each set of coordinates are four different ways to transform the object. For instance, I have drawn chair 1 in the diagram below. Notice that exchanging the x and y coordinates cause the chair to face east instead of north, multiplying the x axis by 2 widens the chair into a sofa, and adding numbers to the x and y coordinates moves it into position. The transformed coordinates are: 1,6,0 → 1,6,2 → 1,10,2 → 1,10,0; 1,6,1 → 1,10,1 → 2,10,1 → 2,6,1 → 1,6,1; 2,6,0 → 2,6,1; 2,10,0 → 2,10,1

Can you draw the other eight objects to complete the living room? Hint: the door sometimes transforms into a window. Answers on page 113.

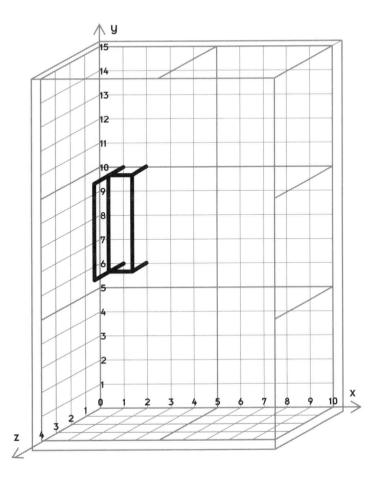

Mental Blocks

H ere is a 3-D puzzle to give your spatial imagination a workout. I used a 3-D modeling program to create the sixteen floating objects at right. Each object is composed of six cubes, all the same size, joined face-to-face to make a single, connected object. Some of the cubes are hidden in back of other cubes, where they cannot be seen, so some of the shapes are ambiguous. For instance, figure P might be either of the two objects shown below.

Can you identify eight different pairs of objects that could have the same shape? Ignore differences in color and texture. For instance, objects 1 and 7 match.

Some objects have more than one potential match—object 2 could match either objects 8 or 10, depending on where the missing cubes are—but in the final analysis, each object can belong to only one pair. Hint: Consider where the hidden cubes might be. Answers on page 113.

"Not merely a chip of the old block, but the old block itself."
—Edmunde Burke

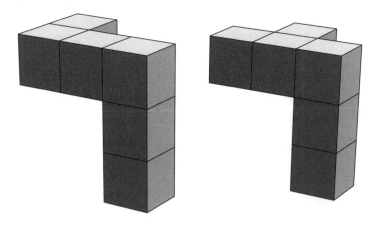

Object 16 could be either of these shapes.

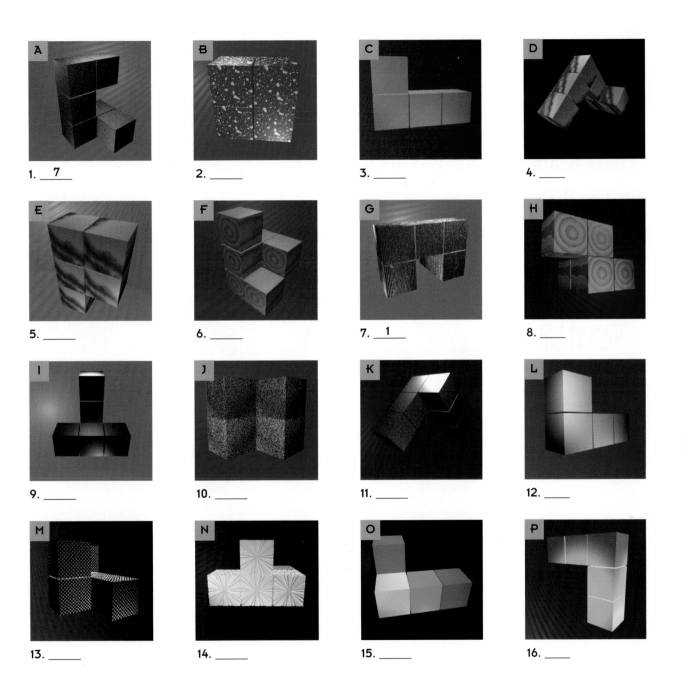

1. __7__

2. _____

3. _____

4. _____

5. _____

6. _____

7. __1__

8. _____

9. _____

10. _____

11. _____

12. _____

13. _____

14. _____

15. _____

16. _____

Me and My Shadow

Designing in three dimensions can be tricky, especially if you are used to working with flat artwork.

Each of the twelve shadows below was cast by one of the twelve objects pictured at right. For instance, shadow No. 1 belongs to the teapot (A). Some shadows look like they could match more than one object. For instance, the circle-shaped shadow might belong to one of several models. However there is only one way to match each shadow with a different object.

Can you match each shadow with its object? Write the letter for the corresponding object below each shadow.

Hint: what does a cube look like if you look straight at a corner? Answers on page 114.

"I have a little shadow that goes in and out with me . . ."
— Robert Louis Stevenson

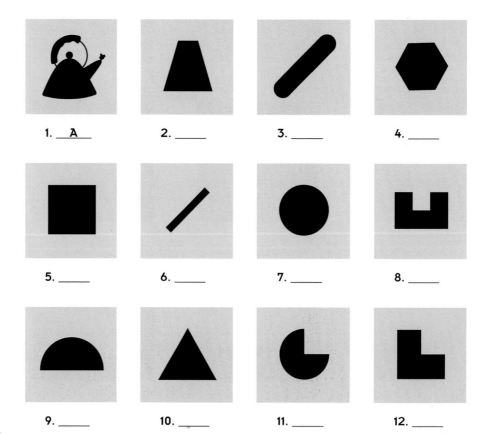

1. __A__   2. _____   3. _____   4. _____

5. _____   6. _____   7. _____   8. _____

9. _____   10. _____   11. _____   12. _____

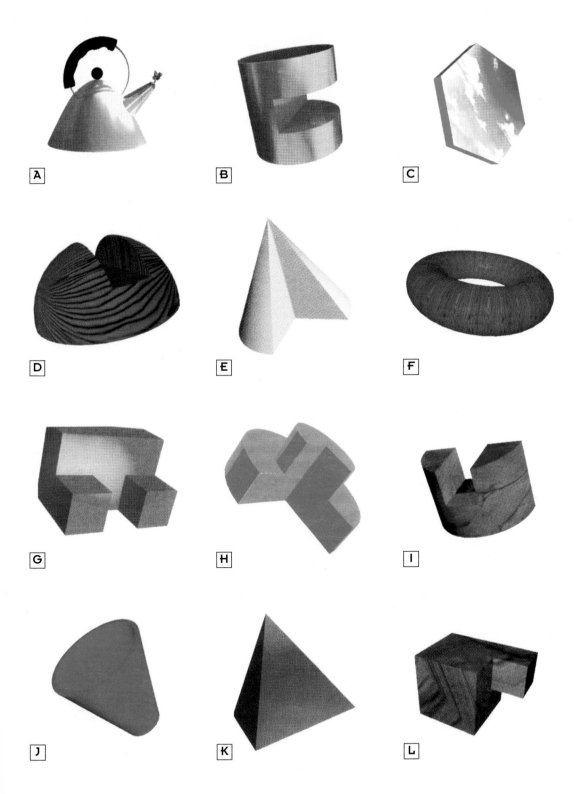

A

B

C

D

E

F

G

H

I

J

K

L

Revolutionary Thinking

"The axis of the earth sticks out visibly through the center of each and every town or city."
—Oliver Wendell Holmes

Notice any unusual similarity between the bottle and the plate shown below? Both were created in the 3-D graphics package, Adobe Dimensions. And both are cylindrical shapes that can be formed on a potter's wheel or lathe. Such shapes are called "surfaces of revolution."

But there is more. If you cut open the two shapes you will see that both were created by spinning cross sections of exactly the same shape (in red) around an axis (the dotted gray line). For instance, the neck of the bottle and the lip of the plate were swept out by the same part of the cross section. The only

difference between the two shapes is that the cross section has been rotated 90 degrees relative to the axis of rotation.

At right are twelve more surfaces of revolution. Six pairs have identical half cross sections. Each cross section is made of just two or three straight lines. Can you match each shape with the other shape that has the same cross-section? For instance, shapes 6 and 10 match. Write your answers in the blanks.

Hint: First find the axis of revolution. Then imagine cutting the object in half down the axis. Draw the cross section revealed by the cut. Answers on page 114.

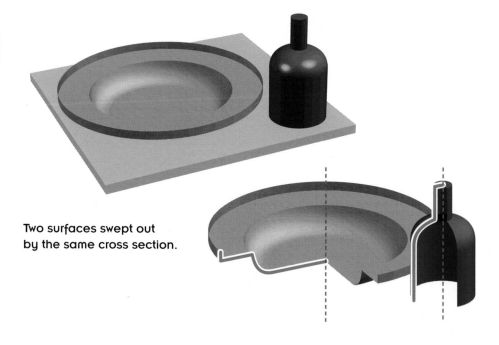

Two surfaces swept out by the same cross section.

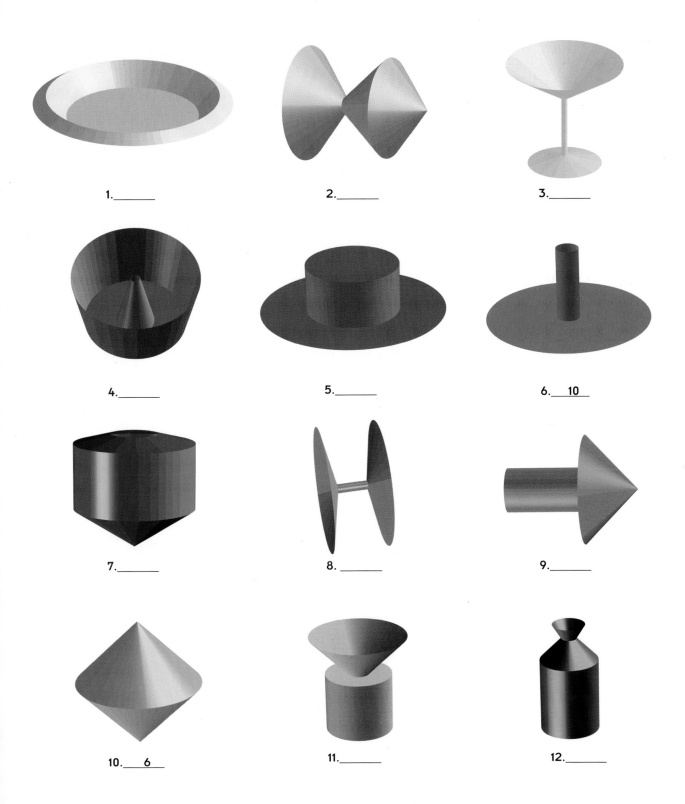

1._____

2._____

3._____

4._____

5._____

6.__10__

7._____

8._____

9._____

10.__6__

11._____

12._____

Point of View

"I am a camera with its shutter open . . ."
—Christopher Isherwood

One of the most exciting uses of computer graphics technology is that it lets you travel through simulated three-dimensional environments. Architects, city planners, and set designers use programs like Virtus WalkThrough to get a feel for their designs even before they are built. Moving points of view are also popular in flight simulators and in computed animated titles.

For years film and TV productions have used 3-D modeling software to create dramatic openings, transitions, and backgrounds. Now multimedia projects are starting to incorporate 3-D computer graphics.

To design for a moving camera, you have to learn to think in three dimensions. I have placed nine cameras in the scene at right. Each snapshot shows the viewpoint of one camera. For instance, the snapshot below was taken by camera F

Can you match each of the other eight snapshots with the corresponding camera? Each camera is used just once. You can assume that some cameras have zoom lenses, so close-up shots may actually have been taken from far away. Write your answers in the blanks at right.

Hint: some snapshots may show areas that are not visible in the big picture. Answers on page 114.

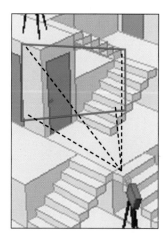

A camera...

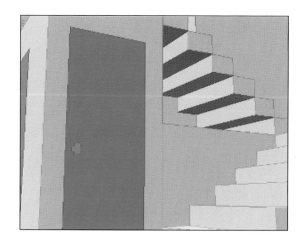

and what it sees.

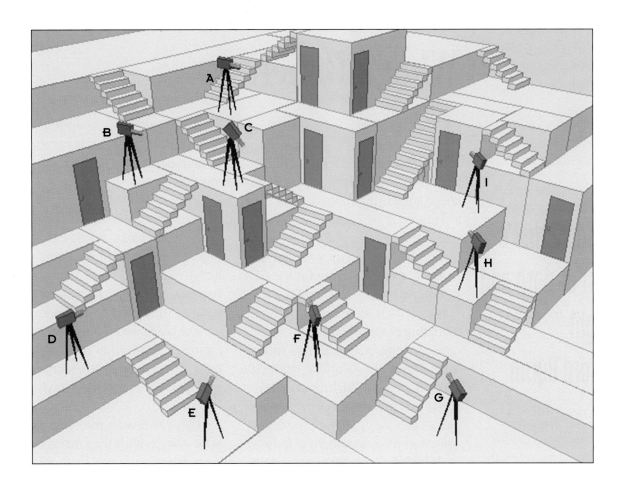

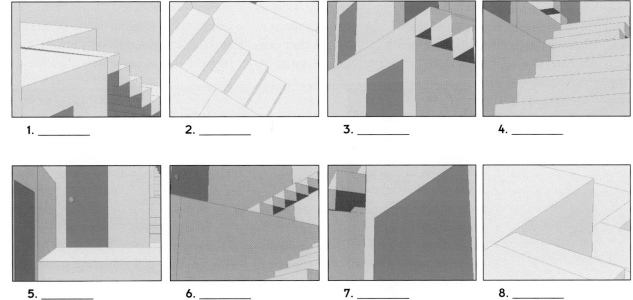

1. _____

2. _____

3. _____

4. _____

5. _____

6. _____

7. _____

8. _____

What a Relief!

> "And all that's best of dark and bright."
> —Lord Byron

Three-dimensional modeling programs make it easy to create geometric forms like cylinders and cubes. But what if you want to create something more organic, like a crumpled blanket or an eroded hillside? The folks at Cyan faced just this problem when they set out to model the island setting for the CD-ROM game Myst. To create the terrain they used the three-dimensional modeling program StrataVision to convert a gray-scale painting into a three-dimensional surface, with light areas mapping to high points and dark areas mapping to low points like a relief map. Then they added color and trees, as shown at below.

John Knoll, co-author of Adobe Photoshop, has created a similar Photoshop plug-in called CyberMesh. CyberMesh converts a gray-scale image into a file that can be read into a three-dimensional modeling program. As with StrataVision, light pixels correspond to high points, and dark pixels to low points.

With CyberMesh, all the Photoshop tools become three-dimensional distortion tools. For instance, Figure A at right shows a gray-scale image of a face. Figure 1 shows the corresponding CyberMesh model. If you use the Invert command to reverse black and white, you get Figure B. Notice that the highs and lows are reversed in the corresponding CyberMesh model, shown in Figure 2.

Can you match the other gray-scale images with the corresponding CyberMesh surfaces? Each image matches just one surface. Write your answers in the blanks. Hint: Check the locations of the lightest and darkest points. Answers on page 114.

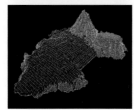

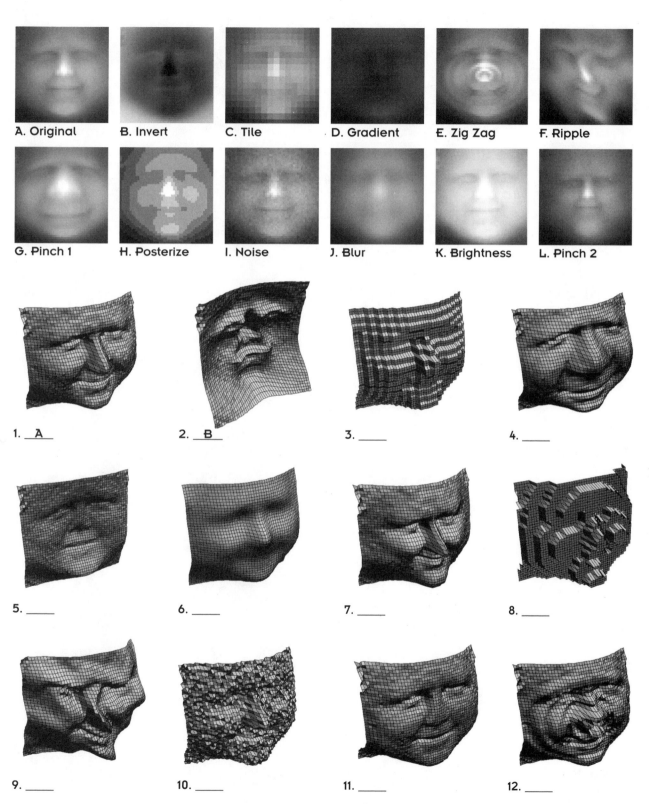

A. Original
B. Invert
C. Tile
D. Gradient
E. Zig Zag
F. Ripple
G. Pinch 1
H. Posterize
I. Noise
J. Blur
K. Brightness
L. Pinch 2

1. __A__
2. __B__
3. _____
4. _____
5. _____
6. _____
7. _____
8. _____
9. _____
10. _____
11. _____
12. _____

CHAPTER 6
Programming

The puzzles in this chapter exercise some of the basic skills of a computer programmer or engineer—the ability to find precise solutions to technical problems.

Lost in HyperText, and Go Non-Linear run you through the mazes of planning software. Get with the Program and In a Class by Itself teach you some of the basics of computer programming. Small, Cheap, or Good? lets you wrestle with some the design tradeoffs that multimedia producers face every day. It Takes All Sorts addresses the common problem of sorting items in a database program. Buzzword Rebus tests your knowledge of multimedia jargon.

To put yourself in a programmer's frame of mind, imagine writing instructions on how to address, stamp, and mail a letter. Your instructions will be read by an extraterrestrial being that understands English but has never seen an envelope or stamp before. Furthermore, you are not allowed to use diagrams, only words. How would you do it? What would be hard? What things would you have to describe that are normally taken for granted? How could you word your instructions so they work for different sizes of envelopes, addresses, and stamps?

The history of computers is like the history of automobiles. In the early days of automobiles, you had to be a mechanic to drive a car. As cars became more common, they got easier to use, and auto repair shops appeared. Similarly, in the early days of computers, you had to be a programmer to use a computer. As personal computers have become more common, they have gotten easier to use, and computer service centers have appeared.

Today, high-level multimedia authoring software like Macromedia Authorware, HyperCard, or Toolbook let nonprogrammers build things that would have taken weeks of expert programming just a few years ago.

Nevertheless it pays for everyone in multimedia to know a bit about programming, just as it pays for everyone who drives to know a bit about auto mechanics. Not only will you be more self-sufficient, you will be able to take advantage of what computers do well, rather than struggle to make computers imitate other media like print or movies.

For excellent nontechnical introductions to computers and programming, see *How Computers Work* and *How Computer Programming Works.*

Lost in Hypertext

> "How many roads must a man walk down before you can call him a man?"
> —Bob Dylan

We read books sequentially from beginning to end. In the new interactive media, we can read non-sequentially, skipping from topic to topic as we choose. Ted Nelson coined the word "hypertext" to refer to any form of non-sequential writing.

It's easy to get lost in hypertext, especially if the links from page to page get complicated. At right is a 16-page hypertext document. From any page you can travel to either of the two pages listed at the bottom of the page. Can you find a way to start on Page 1, visit every page just once, and end on Page 16? Fill in your answers in the blanks.

Hints: From page 1 the next page is 12. Consider which pages you can come from to get to a particular page. You may want to draw a diagram of the connections. Answers on page 115.

Transportation images courtesy of Peoria, Ill.-based Multi-Ad Services Inc. from its ProArt Professional Art Library CD-ROM.

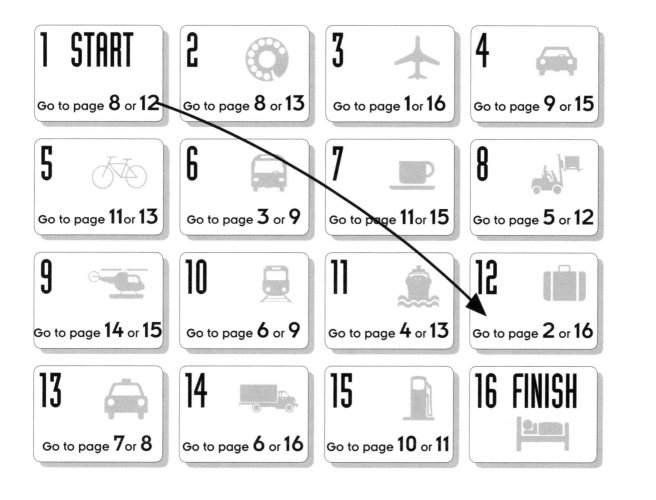

1 START
Go to page **8** or **12**

2
Go to page **8** or **13**

3
Go to page **1** or **16**

4
Go to page **9** or **15**

5
Go to page **11** or **13**

6
Go to page **3** or **9**

7
Go to page **11** or **15**

8
Go to page **5** or **12**

9
Go to page **14** or **15**

10
Go to page **6** or **9**

11
Go to page **4** or **13**

12
Go to page **2** or **16**

13
Go to page **7** or **8**

14
Go to page **6** or **16**

15
Go to page **10** or **11**

16 FINISH

1   12 — — — — — — — — — — — — 16

Small, Cheap or Good?

Get out your spreadsheets!

You have been asked to produce a CD-ROM on the life of J. S. Bach, including elements of music, narration, musical scores, still images, and video clips. Each element can be realized in several formats with different trade-offs in disk space, production cost, and value to users.

To fit all the material on the disc, you must decide when to give up quality to gain space. For instance, a CD-ROM holds only about an hour of music at full CD quality. To fit more music on the disc, your producers have already decided to store some music at lesser quality.

Your challenge is to choose between two different formats for each element so that the complete production stays within the limits of 650 megabytes of disk space and $100,000 of production budget while delivering at least 100 points of value.

Write your choices, A or B, in the six blanks. Check your answers on page 115.

			Mbytes	$1,000s	Value
1. **Higher Quality Music** (19 min.)	A.	**CD-DA** has the same high quality as regular music CDs. About an hour of music fits on a full CD. (For music in this format, 1 sec. = 160K.)	180	10	20
	B.	**Level A Stereo** takes half the space of CD-DA. Twice the music fits in the same space, but quality is lower. (Two hours fit on a CD. 1 sec. = 80K.)	90	10	15
2. **Lower Quality Music** (1.5 hrs.)	A.	**Level B Stereo** takes a quarter the space of CD-DA. Its quality is sig-nifi-cantly lower than that of CD-DA. Four hours fit on a CD. (1 sec. = 40K.)	216	15	14
	B.	**MIDI**, the standard for electronic music. Its quality can be high for some kinds of music. Space is low, but conversion takes work. (1 min. = 5K.)	0.5	35	12
3. **Narration** (6 hrs.)	A.	**Level C Mono** takes a sixteenth the space of CA-DA. Its quality is poor for music, but fine for voice. (Sixteen hours fit on a CD. 1 sec = 10K.)	216	15	18
	B.	**Text** is the most compact format of all. No room for audio narra-tion? Consider text. A thousand 300-page books fit on a CD. (One page = 1K.)	0.3	8	11
4. **Scores** (500 pages)	A.	**Photographs of Scores**, like all proprietary images, cost a lot to license. Licensing costs often eat up CD-ROM budgets. (One page = 200K.)	100	20	20
	B.	**Typeset Scores**, like MIDI and typeset text, take little room to store since the computer remembers symbols, not images. (One page = 20K.)	10	15	15
5. **Images** (500 images)	A.	**Photographic Images** take a lot of space. JPEG can compress a full-color 640 by 480 image to one-tenth its original size. (One image = 100K.)	100	5	20
	B.	**Drawn Images** have solid colors that compress much more efficiently than those in photographs. (A full-screen image may take only 10K.)	10	20	18
6. **Video** (5 min)	A.	**30 Frames per Second** is standard for TV. Digital video often reduces image size to gain time. (1 sec. = 30 frames at 17K/image = 500K.)	150	15	18
	B.	**15 Frames per Second** is common for animation. Flicker is visible, but tolerable;40 min. fit on a CD. (1 sec. = 15 frames at 17K/image = 250K.)	75	15	14
		Totals			

1. _____   2. _____   3. _____   4. _____   5. _____   6. _____

<650   <100   >100

Go Non-Linear

In traditional media like books and movies, the story follows a single linear path to its conclusion. In interactive media, such as CD-ROMs and videogames, the reader can follow different branches of a non-linear "story tree."

Non-linear stories present interesting challenges. The storyteller's challenge is to make choice an integral part of the experience. The producer's challenge is to find a way to show all the possible branches in a tree without exceeding budget or disc space—the total footage for a simple hour-long story with ten, two-way branch points would add up to nearly 200 hours!

There is a technical challenge, too. Mass storage media like CD-ROMs and videodiscs cannot make large skips on a disc without noticeable delay. For instance, a Pioneer videodisc player can play consecutive frames forward or backward smoothly, but must pause to reposition the read head whenever it skips more than 100 frames.

We've taken short clips from the CD-ROM "A Hard Day's Night" by The Voyager Company and composed them as a web of possible paths. There are ten clips, from 1 to 10 frames long. The arrows show the "hypervideo" jumps that must

be possible to complete once the clips are laid out.

Can you arrange the clips so that you never have to skip more than nine frames when jumping from the end of one clip to the beginning of another along the paths indicated by the arrows? Clip 6 must run forward, but all others may run either forward or backward. For instance,

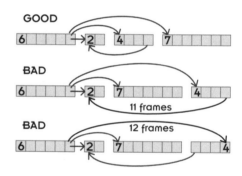

you could order the three clips that can follow Clip 6 as 2, 4, 7, but not 2, 7, 4, because you would have to jump eleven frames to get from the end of clip 4 to the beginning of Clip 2. You can shorten the jump to nine frames by reversing Clip 4, but then the jump from Clip 6 to Clip 4 is too long.

Write your answers in the blanks. Indicate a backward clip by writing a left-pointing arrow above the number. Answers on page 115.

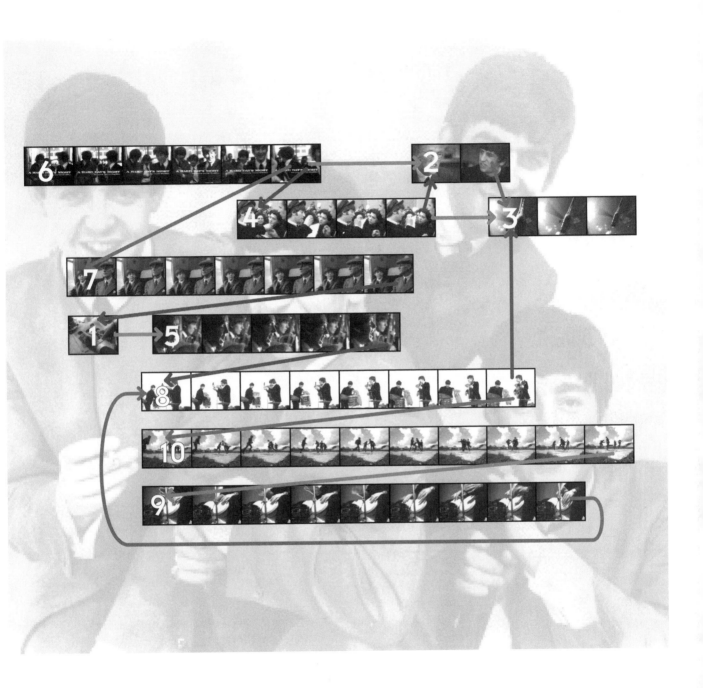

6

Get with the Program

You don't have to be a programmer to figure out this puzzle—but it helps.

If you want your multimedia productions to be more than glorified slideshows, you need to know about programming. Most multimedia authoring tools include programming languages.

A program is a list of instructions. Since computers carry out instructions verbatim, programmers have to be precise. This puzzle will give you a taste of programming. You will need a penny, a nickel, a dime, and a quarter—and a finger.

The five instructions below at left describe ways to rearrange the coins and move your finger from position to position. A list of these instructions makes up a program. For instance, start with the coins in the sequence: dime, penny, quarter, nickel and follow the program ABCDE.

The diagrams in the example below at right show the results of each step. Notice that the finger moves in Step 3, but not in Step 5,

INSTRUCTIONS

A. **BEGIN.** Put your finger on the first (left-most) coin.

B. **MAYBE EXCHANGE.** If your finger is not on the last (right-most) coin, and the coin to the right of your finger is of less value than the coin under it, exchange the "finger" coin with the one to its right and end with your finger at the same position.

C. **MOVE RIGHT.** If your finger is not on the last coin, move your finger one position to the right.

D. **EXCHANGE.** If your finger is not on the last coin, exchange the coin at your finger position with the coin to its right without moving your finger.

E. **MAYBE MOVE RIGHT.** If your finger is not on the last coin, and the coin to the right of your finger is of greater value than the coin under your finger, move your finger one coin to the right.

Example: Program ABCDE

Step 1. (after A):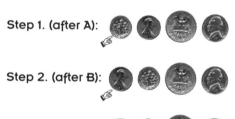

Step 2. (after B):

Step 3. (after C):

Step 4. (after D):

Step 5 (after E):

since Instruction E says to move your finger only if the coin to the right is of greater value.

Below are eight pairs of beginning and ending sequences. Can you match each pair with a program that turns the beginning sequence into the ending sequence?

Write your answers in blanks below. Hint: Each program is used just one time. Check your answers on page 115.

BEGINNING	ENDING	PROGRAM
1. **A**		a. ABC
2. ___		b. ADE CB
3. ___		c. ABC BCB D
4. ___		d. ACC BCB A
5. ___		e. ADC CBA BC
6. ___		f. AEC BAB CDE
7. ___		g. ACC BAE DEC
8. ___		h. ACB EDA CBD

In a Class by Itself

Object-oriented programming, or OOP as it is known, is taking worlds of computers and business by storm. OOP is a style of programming in which all the data and behaviors associated with a single entity like a window are grouped into a single "object," rather than being spread out among several places as they are in older programming languages. Programs written in object-oriented languages like C++ or SmallTalk tend to be easier to write and maintain than programs written in older languages like Pascal or C.

Typical objects include visible interface elements, such as buttons and windows, and invisible operating-system elements, such as files and processes. Objects with similar characteristics are grouped into classes, while a specialized object that occurs often enough gets its own subclass.

For instance, in the NEXTSTEP environment the Open File panel belongs to the class OpenWindow, which is a subclass of Window.

Equivalently, we can say that Window is a superclass of OpenWindow, which is a superclass of the Open File panel.

At right are the names of 12 different types of polygons; some are more specialized than others. For instance, a square is a special kind of rectangle, so Rectangle is a superclass of Square. Your challenge is to draw arrows pointing from each superclass to all of its immediate subclasses. Do not draw extra arrows that skip intermediate subclasses. For instance, you should draw an arrow from Parallelogram to Rectangle and from Rectangle to Square, but not from Parallelogram to Square.

Some classes have more than one superclass (a square is both a rectangle and a rhombus). The marks show which angles and sides are equal.

Hint: A convex polygon has no angle greater than 180 degrees, and a trapezoid has four sides, two of which are parallel. Check your answers on page 116.

"I could have had class. I could have been a contender."
—Marlon Brando in On the Waterfront

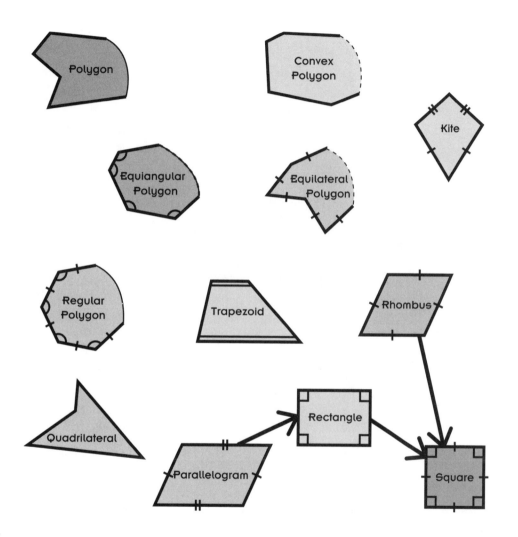

Polygon

Convex Polygon

Kite

Equiangular Polygon

Equilateral Polygon

Regular Polygon

Trapezoid

Rhombus

Quadrilateral

Rectangle

Parallelogram

Square

It Takes All Sorts

"The old order changeth yielding place to new."
—Alfred Lord Tennyson

Every multimedia project needs a way to keep track of the thousands of component sounds, pictures, movies and other media elements that are to be assembled. That is where database programs come in handy.

Here is a little database of "Star Trek: The Next Generation" characters. Notice that all records are visible at once in a single spreadsheet-like table. Each record appears in a separate row, and each field within a record appears in a separate column.

If we sort by first name, we get example A. If we sort by last name, we get example B. If we want to completely alphabetize the names, we need to do a multiple sort by last, then first name, as shown in C.

Example 1 below shows a database of six names from a family from Altair IX. Each record spells a single name reading across, with just one letter per field. As you can see, the names are in alphabetical order.

Example 2 shows the database sorted by third letter. Notice that names with the same third letter stay in the same order they were in before they were sorted. For instance, Bolero stays before Kalero. Example 3 shows the database sorted by third letter, then second letter, then sixth letter, or 326 for short.

A. First name
Beverly	Crusher
Deanna	Troi
Jean Luc	Picard
Wesley	Crusher

B. Last name
Wesley	Crusher
Beverly	Crusher
Jean Luc	Picard
Deanna	Troi

C. Last, then first name
Beverly	Crusher
Wesley	Crusher
Jean Luc	Picard
Deanna	Troi

1. Alphabetical order
B	A	T	U	N	O
B	A	T	U	R	A
B	O	L	E	R	O
K	A	L	E	R	O
K	O	L	U	N	A
K	O	T	E	N	A

2. Sort order: 3
B	O	L	E	R	O
K	A	L	E	R	O
K	O	L	U	N	A
B	A	T	U	N	O
B	A	T	U	R	A
K	O	T	E	N	A

3. Sort order: 326
K	A	L	E	R	O
K	O	L	U	N	A
B	O	L	E	R	O
B	A	T	U	R	A
B	A	T	U	N	O
K	O	T	E	N	A

Can you figure out the sort orders for these five examples? Names stay in alphabetical order if they have the same letter in the field being sorted. Write your answers in the blanks. The number of blanks show how many fields are in each sort. The last two examples each have two possible solutions. Answers on page 116.

6. Sort order: __ __ __

B	A	T	U	N	O
K	O	L	U	N	A
K	O	T	E	N	A
K	A	L	E	R	O
B	A	T	U	R	A
B	O	L	E	R	O

4. Sort order: __ __

K	A	L	E	R	O
B	A	T	U	N	O
B	A	T	U	R	A
B	O	L	E	R	O
K	O	L	U	N	A
K	O	T	E	N	A

7. Sort order: __ __ __ __

K	O	T	E	N	A
K	O	L	U	N	A
B	A	T	U	R	A
B	A	T	U	N	O
K	A	L	E	R	O
B	O	L	E	R	O

5. Sort order: __ __ __

K	A	L	E	R	O
K	O	T	E	N	A
B	O	L	E	R	O
B	A	T	U	N	O
B	A	T	U	R	A
K	O	L	U	N	A

8. Sort order: __ __ __ __

K	A	L	E	R	O
B	O	L	E	R	O
K	O	L	U	N	A
K	O	T	E	N	A
B	A	T	U	R	A
B	A	T	U	N	O

Buzzword Rebus

We've taken sixteen common multimedia buzzwords and dressed them up as rebuses. For instance, the rebus below shows the letter "N" inside "tendo", so the answer is "N-in-tendo", or "Nintendo". Can you decipher the other buzzwords?

Write your answers in the blanks. Some answers are single words or names; others are short phrases. The blanks show how many words appear in each answer. Hint: every buzzword appears somewhere in this book. Answers on page 116.

"Our is the age of substitues: instead of language, we have jargon."
—Eric Bentley

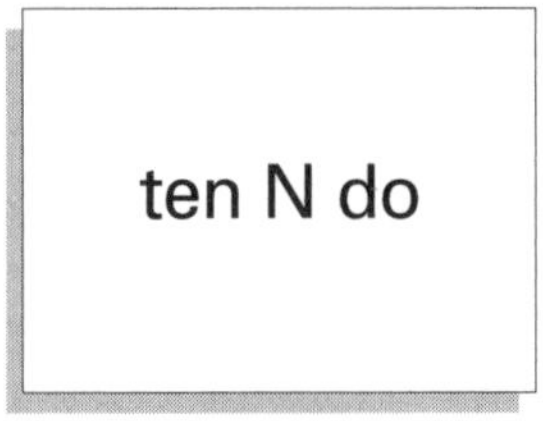

ten N do

Nintendo

1. mul ⊘ dia

1. _____

2. modddeling

2. ____ – ____

3.

3. _____ _____

4. CO|OR (bicycle)

4. _____

5. 8

5. _____ - _____

6. resolution

6. _____ _____

7. text

7. _____

8. SHOT

8. ____ - ____ _____

9. PG

9. _____ _____

10. REVOLUTION

10. _____ _____

11. elbitapmoc

11. _____ _____

12. KILO

12. _____

13. VID (briefcase)

13. _____ _____

14. aud10

14. _____ _____

15. esuom

15. _____ _____

Answers

Chapter 1. Sound

Watching the Months Roll By (page 12)

1. July; 2. October; 3. August; 4. February;
5. March; 6. May; 7. December; 8. April;
9. June; 10. September; 11. January;
12. November

This was my first *NewMedia* puzzle. I chose to do a sound puzzle because of all the topics I wanted to cover, sound seemed to be the hardest to do in print. Here is a letter from someone who analyzed the sound wave. Much of the analysis is correct, but I don't sing in a rock band.

> The speaker who recorded those months is male. He is between 20 and 40 years old. His larynx is in reasonably health, although his vocal folds did not completely smoothly recover from being adducted at the start of "April". (Does he smoke? Or perhaps often shouts at sports matches or sings in a rock band.)
>
> The speaker is probably a native North American, but at any rate did not grow up in the deep south. (Is he from New England?) He has very careful diction, and recorded the words quite close to the microphone in a quiet room with either a computer fan or an air-conditioner in the background. In fact he was TOO close to the microphone during "November," "Graphics", "August," "October," "July," and "September," as is evidenced by the waveform being clipped.
>
> He spoke "computer" and "graphics" as a single phrase (compare the rate of the closing gesture at the end of the last syllable of "computer" to that of "November," note also the low amplitude and low fundamental frequency in the last syllable of "graphics," and he took a deep breath before doing so (note the second syllable of "computer" has the highest fundamental frequency in all his speech).
>
> — Kim Silverman, White Plains, New York

Parts of Speech (page 14)

1. Hollywood; 2. mouse; 3. click; 4. bugs;
5. monitor; 6. compression; 7. times; 8. Users;
9. ship; 10. backed up; 11. standards

The Third Wave (page 16)

2. A+D; 3. B+C; 4. C+F; 5. B+E; 6. D+E;
7. E+F; 8. C+D; 9. A+D+F; 10. A+B+C;
11. D+E+F; 12. B+C+F

In puzzle 2, two waves add up to zero. In general, any sound wave and its opposite add up to silence. This leads to an interesting question: could you make a device that creates silence by emitting the opposite of whatever sound it receives? Here's an unsolved challenge: can you draw a wave like the ones in the puzzle that you cannot make by adding some combination of waves A–F?

Lip Sync (page 18)

1. C; 2. E; 3. G; 4. D; 5. I; 6. A; 7. J; 8. F;
9. H; 10. B; 11. Read my lips

Several speech therapists sent in the answers to Lip Sync and seemed to make easy work of it. Other readers did this puzzle with their children.

Music to My Eyes (page 20)

1. B; 2. G; 3. A; 4. L; 5. D; 6. J; 7. B; 8. E;
9. F; 10. K; 11. I; 12. C

Denys Parsons compiled a fascinating book called *The Directory of Tunes and Musical Themes*, now out of print, that indexes melodies entirely by whether the next note in the melody is higher, lower or a repeat of the previous note. For instance, the beginning of Frére Jacques is written as *UUD RUUD UUU DUU — the first note is always written as an asterisk, U means up, D means down, and R means repeat.

Surprisingly most melodies can be uniquely identified in about ten notes, only a few more than the number of notes needed in a conventional melody dictionary, which indexes melodies by the names of the notes once the melody is transposed to C Major or a minor.

Here is a comment from a NewMedia reader:

After spending a few years working with amateur MIDI quipment, it's interesting to notice that you can actually get used to looking at this sort of music notation. Coming from a computer background and having very little training in "classical" music notation, in general I find it far simpler to comprehend (though I'm painfully aware of some of its limitations).

—Gabriel Lawrence, Burlington, Massachusetts

Format Maze (page 22)

J. 8; H. 8; F. 8; B. 9; I. 8; C. 4; G. 3; D. 8

Sounds Like (page 24)

1. F; 2. J; 3. E; 4. N; 5. I; 6. K; 7. M; 8. P;
9. A; 10. H; 11. D; 12. G; 13. B; 14. L; 15. Q;
16. C; 17. O

In researching this puzzle I found that very little has been written about how Foley artists work. Most are quite protective of their techniques. Special thanks to Allison Moore for her generosity sharing her knowledge.

Chapter 2. Graphics

Counter Proposal (page 28)

A. 23; B. 14; C. 16; D. 24; E. 7; F. 13; G. 9;
H. 5; I. 20; J. 22; K. 2; L. 4; M. 18; N. 6;
O. 10; P. 8; Q. 21; R. 3; S. 19; T. 17; U. 12;
V. 26; W. 15; X. 11; Y. 1; Z. 25

Look on the Bright Side (page 30)

1. A; 2. G; 3. E; 4. J; 5. C; 6. H; 7. L; 8. K;
9. F; 10. I; 11. B; 12. D

Several readers solved this puzzle by scanning the page into Adobe Photoshop, then using the Histogram feature to measure the percentage of black pixels in the overall image. That happens to be the way that I ranked the images when I created the puzzle, except that the images started on screen instead of on paper.

Out of Proportion (page 32)

1. A; 2. C; 3. F; 4. H; 5. G; 6. K; 7. L; 8. J;
9. B; 10. D; 11. E; 12. I

The ratio used for index cards—3 to 5, 4 to 6 and 5 to 8—is an approximation of the golden ratio (1.618...), which ancient Greeks and other mathematically inclined aestheticians have considered the most pleasing proportion for a rectangle. For instance, the front of the Parthenon is in the golden ratio.

The proportion used by European stationery is a close approximation of the square root of 2. This proportion has the special property that if you fold a piece of paper in half you get a rectangle with the same proportions as the original; if you fold 8.5" by 11" paper in half you get a rectangle that has taller proportions.

For more on the history of wide screen movies, see the fascinating book *Wide Screen Movies*. In practice, the actual proportions of movies in movie theaters vary quite a bit, since movies are normally projected larger than the screen area, with the overflow projected onto black nonreflrective areas. Similarly, TV screens typically overscan the picture slightly larger than the active tube area, so some of the edge of the picture is lost.

RGB Mixup (page 34)

5. RG; 6. RB; 7. GB; 8. GRB; 9. BGR; 10. BRG; 11. GBR; 12. RBG

You might wonder why books and computer screens use different systems of colored dots to produce color. If you look closely at a printed color page such as the ones in this book, you will not see red, green, and blue dots, but red, yellow, blue, and black dots. Printers call these colors magenta (red), yellow, cyan (green-blue), and black, and often use the single-letter abbreviations C, M, Y, and K (last letter of "black").

Why are books and magazines printed with four colors of ink, when black can be printed as a mixture of magenta, yellow, and cyan? Why are books printed in magenta, yellow, and cyan inks, when our eyes are sensitive to red, green, and blue light?

To answer the first question: printers use four inks instead of three because the majority of printed material is words, which are normally printed in black. Black can also be printed as a mixture of magenta, yellow and cyan, but words printed this way tend to look fuzzy at the edges because the printing plates will usually misalign slightly. Also, the black produced by black ink tends to be darker than the black produced by overprinting magenta, yellow, and cyan.

The answer to the second question is that printers use cyan, magenta, and yellow instead of red, green, and blue because inks on paper mix colors differently from pixels on computers. Reflective media like ink on paper work by subtracting colors from white light, whereas luminous media like computer screens work by adding colored light to darkness. For instance, adding magenta, yellow, and cyan inks gives you black; while adding red, green, and blue lights gives you white.

The primary colors for subtractive media are the exact complements of the primary colors for additive media: magenta is white minus green; yellow is white minus blue; and cyan is white minus red. The two color systems are not really different, but are two sides of the same coin.

Filter Fantasies (page 36)

1. CA; 2. DCB; 3. FEA; 4. EDC; 5. ABC; 6. BDF

Worf Morph (page 38)

1. HI; 2. DG; 3. CJ; 4. BF; 5. AE; 6. AD; 7. FI; 8. HJ; 9. BG; 10. FHI; 11. DGJ; 12. BCE

You can see Nancy Burson's fascinating and often politically minded morphs in her book *Composites*. Pictures of missing children are often electronically aged by morphing a picture of the child with a picture of an older relative.

Package Deal (page 40)

1. A; 2. K; 3. D; 4. F; 5. L; 6. J; 7. G; 8. H; 9. C; 10. I; 11. C; 12. B; 13. L; 14. D; 15. B; 16. G; 17. K; 18. A; 19. E; 20. H; 21. F; 22. E; 23. J; 24. I

Chapter 3. Motion

In Transition (page 44)

1. DAF; 2. DFC; 3. BCA; 4. DECB; 5. AFCE;
6. EAFBD

Puzzles about arranging things in time tend to be harder than puzzles about arranging things in space. This puzzle, Get in the Swing, and Going Around in Cycles proved quite difficult for *NewMedia* readers.

Around the Rainbow (page 46)

1–2; 2–1; 3–10; 4–15; 5–7; 6–12; 7–5; 8–13;
9–11; 10–3; 11–9; 12–6; 13–8; 14–16; 15–4;
16–14

If you want to create color cycling effects in MacroMedia Director, consider the XObject called ColorGenie.

The company TECNATION DIGITAL WORLD sells hardware and software for doing color cycling graphics to music, both for home and for night clubs. Their address is listed in the bibliography.

Who's in Front? (page 48)

F G U S Y R K C H X O J M
E W L N A P T Q D Z I B V

Get in the Swing (page 50)

1. F; 2. C; 3. E; 4. B; 5. A; 6. D
7. C; 8. B; 9. F; 10. A; 11. D; 12. E
13. E; 14. D; 15. B; 16. C; 17. F; 18. A

Going Around in Cycles (page 52)

2. DCAEB; 3. EBDAC; 4. DCEBA; 5. BCEAD;
6. CAEDB; 7. ADCEB

The flying bird was taken from the book *Horses & Other Animals in Motion* by Eadweard Muybridge. Note that the downstroke is much longer than the upstroke.

You Call the Shots (page 54)

1. B, V; 2. I, W; 3. L, R; 4. E, X; 5. D, P;
6. G, Q; 7. C, U; 8. J, S; 9. F, M; 10. K, T;
11. H, N; 12. A, O

Thanks to Greg Rickman, who teaches film at San Francisco State University, for helping me call the shots. For a detailed visual analysis of *It's a Wonderful Life*, see *A Certain Tendency of the Hollywood Cinema, 1930–1980*.

Halfway Olympics (page 56)

1. BD 2. EJ 3. FG 4. HI
5. DI 6. CF 7. GH 8. CJ
9. AE 10. FD 11. AB 12. BJ

Some possible names for the combined events:

1. Running Fence; 2. Underwater Cycling;
3. Spike Dunk; 4. Hand Soccer; 5. Shish Kebob;
6. Knockout Ball; 7. Foot Basket Ball;
8. Knockoff; 9. Wet Floor Work;
10. Volley Garde; 11. 100-yard Arabesque;
12. Fast Track

Chapter 4. Interaction

A Likely Story (page 60)

1. A; 2. D; 3. J; 4. B; 5. L; 6. F; 7. C; 8. G; 9. H; 10. K; 11. E; 12. I; 13. M

I drew the diagram without any story in mind, then gave it to Larry Kay to fill in. Larry found writing the story to fit the diagram an interesting challenge. You might enjoy writing another branching story that fits the diagram.

   Originally my diagram did not include node 2. Larry added node 2 featuring Skinny Marv to force paragraph B to be in node 3. Otherwise nodes 3 and 4 would be interchangeable. Can you rewrite nodes 3 and 4 so node 2 is not needed? Nodes 3 and 4 must both be able to be followed by 5, but only 4 can be followed by 6.

A Matter of Interpretation (page 62)

1.	private–eye	A	see (sea)–horse
2.	family–tree	G	palm–reader
3.	birth–right	I	hand–out
4.	pig–pen	O	write (right)–handed
5.	grand–sun (son)	B	hot–dog
6.	cold–duck	K	bird–seed
7.	head–cold	L	snow–job
8.	may–flower	E	rose–hips
9.	hand–bell	N	ring–side
10.	rapid–fire	H	match–box
11.	chain–mail	D	letter–head
12.	half–time	M	watch–band
13.	hair–spray	P	can–opener
14.	race–car	J	auto–graph
15.	board–walk	F	prints (prince)–charming
16.	white–water	C	sea (see)–saw

This puzzle, oddly enough, started with the quotation. My editor Gillian Newson told me she had a quotation from Lewis Carroll that she liked. I took that as a challenge, and came up with a puzzle to match the quotation.

Process of Elimination (page 64)

1. I; 2. K; 3. T; 4. C; 5. M; 6. G; 7. N; 8. Q; 9. E; 10. J; 11. O; 12. R; 13. F; 14. L; 15. P; 16. H; 17. D; 18. B; 19. S; 20. A

It is common for graphic designers to go through hundreds of sketches like these before settling on one solution. The same September 1993 issue of *NewMedia* Magazine which included this puzzle also included an article by Alben & Faris about their design process.

   Special kudos to Janice Justice's 39 students at Gwinnett Vocational Center in Lawrenceville, Georgia who tackled this puzzle in class.

   You may want to try designing your own versions of the icons. Here are versions submitted by Troy Harrison of Big Hand Productions, Dallas, TX:

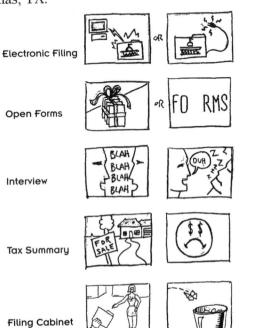

An Eye for an Icon (page 66)

1. A; 2. B; 3. I; 4. O; 5. K; 6. G; 7. L; 8. J;
9. H; 10. C; 11. E; 12. M; 13. N; 14. D; 15. F

The Scarlet Letter (page 68)

Upper Case, Lower Case

Medium Gray, Light Gray

Black, Dark Gray

A, B

Right Side Up, Upside Down

Roman, Italic

The maximum number of two-state controls that you can uniquely identify with four screen shots is eight. With five screen shots you can identify sixteen controls, with six screen shots you can identify thirty two, and so on.

The State of the Button (page 70)

1. A; 2. H; 3. D; 4. G; 5. B; 6. I; 7. E; 8. C;
9. F

Using state transition tables to analyze human-computer interactions is a hot topic among user interface researchers. Michael Chen of Apple Computer wrote an article on the subject called *A Framework for Describing Interactions with Graphical Widgets Using State-Transition Diagrams.*

Once a Pong a Time (page 56)

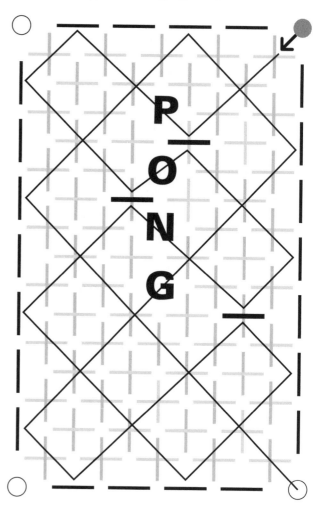

This puzzle has many solutions. Ahmet Nejat Ozsu wrote to tell us that there are 95 solutions out of 410,040 possibilites. The solution above has the maximum number of bounces: 17.

Chapter 5. 3-D

In-Depth Study (page 76)

"TWO EYES ARE BETTER THAN ONE."

I wrote my own program in HyperCard to create this stereogram. If you want to create your own single-image random dot stereograms, try Kai's Power Tools or Stereolusions.

Here is an letter from a *NewMedia* reader who uses random dot stereograms to relax:

> There is a neat, romantic story behind these "SIRDS." I have been interested in SIRDS (Single Image Random Dot Stereography) for several years now. I became engaged to a marvelous guy (first marriage for both of us; I'm 42; he's 53) and I swore I would not marry him until he was capable of the relaxation techniques required to see these! Well, he tried very hard (that was the problem) and I, of course, would not put off getting married just because he couldn't see them! (so much for my willpower!) In any event, I got him a 1-month anniversary present of a book of the SIRDS. Needless to say, he quickly saw the "colorized" types and he's been soooo RELAXED since then.

— Suzanne R. MacTaggart, Stockton, California

Coordinated Effort (page 78)

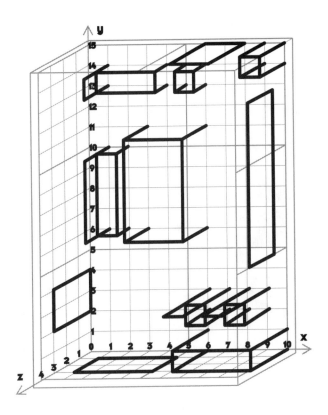

Mental Blocks (page 80)

A–G, B–H, C–K, D–P, E–L, F–M, G–A, H–B, I–O, J–N, K–C, L–E, M–F, N–J, O–I, P–D

This puzzle was inspired by the first NeXT machine, which was a perfect one-foot cube.

Me and My Shadow (page 82)

1. A; 2. J; 3. F; 4. L; 5. K; 6. C; 7. B;
8. I; 9. D; 10. E; 11. H; 12. G.

I always dread the possibility of errors creeping into my puzzles. But sometimes I get lucky. When this puzzle was first published in *NewMedia* magazine, shadow 8 (the square U) was accidentally printed as a copy of shadow 11 (the three-quarters circle). Here are the shadows as they were first printed:

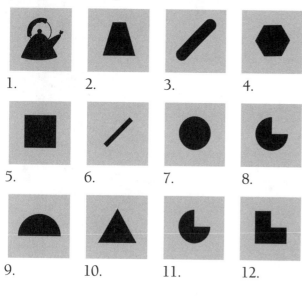

Fortunately this puzzle also has a solution; four to be exact:

1. A; 2. J; 3. F; 4. L; 5. B; 6. C; 7. D; 8. E/H;
9. I; 10. K; 11. H/E; 12. G.

1. A; 2. J; 3. F; 4. L; 5. I; 6. C; 7. B; 8. E/H; 9.
D; 10. K; 11. H/E; 12. G.

Thanks to Eduardo Llach of Acuris for help rendering these illustrations.

Revolutionary Thinking (page 84)

1–12; 2–5; 3–7; 4–8; 5–2; 6–10; 7–3; 8–4;
9–11; 10–6; 11–9; 12–1

When this puzzle first went to press in *NewMedia* magazine, the dotted lines in the example illustration had been accidentally omitted. Fortunately one of the people at the printing house, who was a faithful reader of the puzzle, spotted the problem before it went to press, and he was able to strip in a last minute correction. Talk about service!

Point of View (page 86)

1. F; 2. A; 3. C; 4. G; 5. E; 6. D; 7. H; 8. I;
9. B

I built this model in Virtus Walkthrough, then positioned my point of view at each of the camera sites to determine the best camera angle. When this puzzle first appeared, Virtus Corporation offered a free copy of the Virtus Walkthrough file I created.

What a Relief (page 88)

3. C; 4. K; 5. D; 6. J; 7. L; 8. H; 9. F;
10. H; 11. I; 12. E

CyberMesh was first shown to me by multimedia journalist and designer David Biedne.

Chapter 6. Programming

Lost in HyperText (page 92)

12, 2, 8, 5, 1, 3, 7, 11, 4, 15, 10, 9, 14, 6, 3, 16

Ted Nelson's vision of hypertext would link all the world's literature into a single network. You can read more about his ideas in his book *Computer Lib—Dream Machines*.

Small, Cheap, or Good? (page 94)

1. A; 2. B; 3. B; 4. A; 5. A; 6. A

I worked out the numbers for this puzzle using a spreadsheet; many readers solved it using a spreadsheet. Now that I am involved in CD-ROM authoring I find myself coming face to face with the dilemmas illustrated by this puzzle.

Go Non-Linear (page 96)

←7, 1, 6, 2, 5, 4, 3, 8, ←9, 10

Mark Brown of Costa Mesa, CA figured out that there are ten different solutions to this puzzle, subject to the condition that clip 6 goes forward. Of the ten solutions, nine have clip 6 in position 3. Here is the unique solution that does not have clip 6 in position 3:

←10, 9, ←8, ←3, ←5, ←4, ←2, 1, 6, ←7

This puzzle was inspired by the Aspen Movie Map project. The project, created in 1980 at MIT's Media Lab (then the Architecture Machine Group), is a videodisc-based journey down every street of Aspen, Colorado. At every intersection you can decide to turn left, turn right, or go straight by touching icons along the bottom of the screen. Michael Naimark, one of the creators of the Aspen Movie Map, calls this effect "surrogate travel," an experience he continues to develop at Interval Research in Palo Alto California.

To accomplish the effect of surrogate travel, a camera crew drove down every street in Aspen and made every possible turn (actually, some of the turns were synthesized after the fact by post-processing still images). The video segments were then recorded to videodisc.

Since videodisc players take a few seconds to switch from one part of the disk to another, the authors had to be clever about how the video was laid out on the disk. The Aspen Movie Map uses two videodisc players connected to a single monitor by a computer-controlled video switcher. As one videodisc plays what you see as you drive down the street, the other videodisc repositions the play head at the next intersection, ready to show a left or right turn.

If you choose to go straight, the first videodisc player continues to play straight ahead. If you choose to turn left, the second videodisc player switches in and begins to play.

Now here is the technique that inspired this puzzle. Naimark tells me it was planned but never actually implemented. If you choose to turn right, the second videodisc player switches in and begins to play, but backwards. Both the left turn sequence and right turn sequence begin with the same frame looking straight ahead, so the two sequences could be grafted together by reversing the right turn sequence and splicing it onto the left turn sequence.

Nowadays multimedia authors favor CD-ROMs over videodiscs, but authors still face problems sequencing materials on disk to minimize delays during playback.

Get with the Program (page 98)

1. A; 2. D; 3. B; 4. G; 5. E; 6. C; 7. H; 8. F

We didn't receive one wrong answer to "Get With the Program" but we did get reams of programming code in C, GFA BASIC, Visual BASIC and FORTRAN. One programming teacher even used the puzzle with students.

In a Class by Itself (page 100)

Polygon: Quadrilateral, Equilateral Polygon, Convex Polygon;

Convex Polygon: Equiangular Polygon, Trapezoid, Kite;

Equiangular Polygon: Regular Polygon, Rectangle;

Equilateral Polygon: Regular Polygon, Rhombus;

Kite: Rhombus;

Regular Polygon: Square;

Trapezoid: Parallelogram;

Rhombus: Square;

Quadrilateral: Trapezoid, Kite;

Parallelogram: Rhombus, Rectangle;

Rectangle: Square;

Square: none.

References

A Hard Day's Night (Macintosh CD-ROM). The Voyager Company, 578 Broadway, New York NY 10012. (800) 446-2001.

Acuris, makers of Acuris ClipModels®. 931 Hamilton Ave., Menlo Park, CA 94025. (800) OK-ACURIS.

Adobe Dimensions, Adobe Illustrator, Adobe Photoshop (Windows, Macintosh, SGI, NeXT). Adobe Systems Incorporated, 1585 Charleston Road, Mountain View, California 94039-7900.

Apple Computer. *Electronic Guide to Macintosh® Human Interface Design*. Addison Wesley, 1994. ISBN 0-201-40916-X.

BioVision. Makers of 3-D motion capture systems. 2882 Sand Hill Road, Suite 116, Menlo Park CA 94025. (800) 866-3463.

Bright Star Technology Inc.. Makers of software technology for animated talking characters, including interFACE (Macintosh). 1450 114th Ave., S.E., Suite 200, Bellevue WA 98004. (800) 695-1860.

Burger, Jeff. *The Desktop Multimedia Bible*. Addison Wesley, 1993. ISBN 0-201-58112-4.

Burson, Nancy; Carling, Richard; Kramlich, David. *Composites*. Beach Tree Books, William Morrow, 1986. ISBN 0-688-02601-X.

Carr, Robert E., and Hayes, R. M. *Wide Screen Movies: A History and Filmography of Wide Gauge Filmmaking*. McFarland & Company 1988. ISBN 0-89950-242-3.

Chen, Michael. *A Framework for Describing Interactions with Graphical Widgets Using State-Transition Diagrams* in *Short Papers, InterCHI, 1993*, ACM, 1993. A-W ISBN 0-201-58884-6.

Cinemation (Macintosh). Vividus Corp., 651 Kendall Ave., Palo Alto CA 94306. (415) 321-2221.

ColorGenie. Media Lab, 400 S. McCaslin Blvd., #211, Louisville, CO 80027, (303) 499-5411, (303) 655-0827 (fax).

Cotton, Bob; Oliver, Richard. *Understanding Hypermedia*. Phaidon Press Ltd, 1993. ISBN 0-7148-2809-9.

Cyan. Myst. Broderbund, P. O. Box 6125, Novato, CA 94948-6125.

CyberMesh (Macintosh). Knoll Software, P.O. Box 6887, San Rafael CA 94903. (415) 453-2471.

Dale Seymour Publications, publisher and distributor of educational books on visual thinking, mathematics, and language. P.O. Box 10888, Palo Alto, CA 94303. (415) 324-2800.

DeluxePaint (Window). Electronic Arts.

Director (Windows, Macintosh). MacroMedia, 600 Townsend Street, San Francisco CA 94103. (800) 288-4797.

Edwards, Betty. *Drawing on the Right Side of the Brain*. J. P. Tarcher, 1989. ISBN 0-87477-523-X.

Flow Phazer (Macintosh). NuTopia Inc., 300 Valley St., Suite 302, Sausalito CA 94965.

Foley, James D.; Van Dam, Andries; Feiner, Steven K.; Hughes, John F.; Phillips, Richard L. *Introduction to Computer Graphics.* Addison Wesley 1994. ISBN 0-201-60921-5.

Gardner, Howard. *Frames of Mind.* Basic Books, 1985. ISBN 0-465-02508-0.

Horton, William. *The Icon Book.* John Wiley & Sons, 1993. ISBN 0-471-59901-8.

Interactions. Journal published by ACM, 1515 Broadway, New York NY 10036-5701.

Interactive Entertainment Design. Chris Crawford, 5251 Sierra Road, San Jose, CA 95132

Jerram, Peter; Gosney, Michael. *Multimedia Power Tools.* Random House, 1993. ISBN 0-679-79118-3.

Kai's Power Tools (Windows, Macintosh). HSC Software, 1661 Lincoln Blvd., Suite 101, Santa Monica CA 90404. (310) 392-8441.

Kasdan, Margo A.; Saxton, Christine. *The Critical Eye: An Introduction to Looking at the Movies.* Kendall/Hunt, 1988. ISBN 0-8403-8593-5

Kay, Larry. Writer for interactive media. Toonsmiths, 15466 Los Gatos Blvd., Suite 109, Los Gatos CA 95032.

Laurel, Brenda. *The Art of Human-Computer Interaction Design.* Addison Wesley, 1990. ISBN 0-201-51797-3.

Laybourne, Kit. *The Animation Book.* Crown Trade Paperbacks, 1979. ISBN 0-517-52946-7.

MacInTax (Macintosh). ChipSoft Corp., P.O. Box 85709, San Diego, CA 92186-9668.

MasterTracks (Windows, Macintosh). Passport Designs, Inc., 100 Stone Pine Rd., Half Moon Bay, CA 94019.

McKim, Robert. *Experiences in Visual Thinking.* PWS, 1995.

Morph (Macintosh). Gryphon Software, 7220 Trade St., Suite 120, San Diego CA 92121. (619) 536-8815.

Muybridge, Eadweard. *Horses & Other Animals in Motion.* Dover Publications. 0-486-24911-5.

Nelson, Theodor. *Computer Lib—Dream Machines.* Tempus, Microsoft Press, 1987. ISBN 0-914845-49-7.

NewMedia Magazine, 901 Mariner's Island Blvd., Suite 365, San Mateo, CA 94404. Subscriptions: (609) 786-4430.

Norman, Don. *The Design of Everyday Things.* Doubleday, 1990. ISBN 0-385-26774-6.

Parsons, Denys. *The Directory of Tunes and Musical Themes.* Spencer Brown, 1975. ISBN 0-904747-00-X

Pierce, John. *The Science of Musical Sound.* W. H. Freeman and Company, 1982. ISBN 0-7167-6005-3.

Playmation (Windows, Macintosh). Anjon & Assoc. 714 E. Angeleno, Unit C, Burbank, CA 91501. (818) 566-8551.

Pohlmann, Ken C. *Principles of Digital Audio.* Howard W. Sams & Company, 1989. ISBN 0-672-22634-0.

ProArt Professional Art Library CD-ROM. Multi-Ad Services Inc., 1720 Detweiller Drive, Peoria, IL 61615-1695.

Ray, Robert B. *A Certain Tendency of the Hollywood Cinema 1930–1980.* Princeton University Press, 1985. ISBN 0-691-04727-8.

Sayles, John. *Thinking in Pictures.* Houghton Mifflin, 1987. ISBN 0-395-45388-7.

Seize the Day (DOS, Macintosh). Seize the Day, P.O. Box 833, 3380 Highway 128, Calistoga, CA 94515.

Stereogram. Cadence Books, 1994. ISBN 0-929279-85-9.

Stereolusions (Windows). I/O Software Inc., 10970 Arrow Rte, Cucamonga, CA 91730. (909) 483-5700.

Stratavision 3d. Strata Inc., 2 W. St. George Blvd., Ancestor Square, Suite 2100, St. George, UT 84770. (801) 628-5218.

Synergy. Creators of live color cycling graphics for night clubs and music performances. 22 Russ St., San Francisco, CA 94103.

TECNATION DIGITAL WORLD, makers of Sonovista™ for live visual effects synchronized to music. 555 Bryant St., #257, Palo Alto CA 94301.

Tufte, Edward. *Envisioning Information.* Graphics Press, 1990. ISBN 0-9613921-1-8.

Tully, Tim, and Lehrman, Paul. *MIDI for the Professional.* Amsco Publications, 1993. ISBN 0-8256-1284-5.

Video Toaster. NewTek Inc., 1201 SW Executive Dr., Topeka KS 66615. (800) 843-8934.

Virtus WalkThrough. Virtus Corp. 117 Edinburgh S., Suite 204, Cary NC 27511. (919) 467-9700. Mac.

Vision (Macintosh). Opcode Systems, Inc., 3950 Fabian Way, Suite 100, Palo Alto, CA 94303.

Visual Basic (Windows). Microsoft Corporation, One Microsoft Way, Redmond, WA 98052-6399.

Wilde, Richard. *Problems: Solutions, Visual Thinking for Graphic Communicators.* Van Nostrand Reinhold, 1986. ISBN 0-442-29182-5.

Woolsey, Dr. Kristina Hooper; Curtis, Gayle; Kim, Scott. *VizAbility* (book plus Windows or Macintosh CD-ROM). PWS, 1995.

About the Author

Scott Kim is the author of *Inversions,* a collection of illusionary lettering that reads upside down or in a mirror. His puzzles have appeared in such magazines as *Scientific American, Games, Omni, Discover, NewMedia,* and *NeXTWORLD.* He has designed puzzles for *Heaven & Earth* and other computer games, and worked on software design for Roger von Oech's *Creative Whack Pack* and the forthcoming CD-ROM *VizAbility.* He has a B.A. in music and a Ph.D. in Computers and Graphic Design from Stanford University. He is currently choreographing and performing educational dances about mathematics for schools.

You can write to Scott at:
NewMedia Magazine
901 Mariners Island Blvd, Suite 301
San Mateo CA 94404
415-573-5170
Fax: 415-573-5171
Email: scottkim@aol.com

Other works by Scott Kim:

Inversions Poster Set. Dale Seymour Publications, 1984. P. O. Box 10888, Palo Alto, California, 94303. (800) 872-1100

Inversions. W. H. Freeman & Company, 1989.

Letterforms & Illusion (Macintosh). With Robin Samelson. W. H. Freeman and Company, 1989.

Heaven & Earth (DOS or Macintosh). By Publishing International. Buena Vista Software, 1992.

Creative Whack Pack (Windows or Macintosh). By Roger von Oech. Creative Think, 1993. P. O. Box 7354, Menlo Park, CA, 94026. (415) 321-6775.

VizAbility (CD-ROM and book; Windows or Macintosh). With Dr. Kristina Hooper Woolsey and Gayle Curtis. PWS, 1995.